Private Peaceful

by
Michael Morpurgo

dramatised by
Simon Reade

Resource Material by
Cecily O'Neill

William Collins' dream of knowledge for all began with the publication of his first book in 1819. A self-educated mill worker, he not only enriched millions of lives, but also founded a flourishing publishing house. Today, staying true to this spirit, Collins books are packed with inspiration, innovation and a practical expertise. They place you at the centre of a world of possibility and give you exactly what you need to explore it.

Collins. Do more.

Published by Collins
An imprint of HarperCollins*Publishers*
77–85 Fulham Palace Road
Hammersmith
London
W6 8JB

Commissioned by Charlie Evans
Design by JPD
Cover design by Paul Manning
Production by Arjen Jansen
Printed and bound by Martins the Printers

Browse the complete Collins catalogue at www.collinseducation.com

Acknowledgements

Photo credits: pp 102, 107, 109, 120, 124 Empics/PA Photos; p125 The Defence Picture Library.

Text credits: p107, "Pluck" by Eva Dobell appears by permission of Patrick Dobell, literary editor for Eva Dobell; pp111–114, extracts from the court martial of Harry Farr are reproduced with permission of www.shotatdawn.org.uk and are available from the Public Record Office, file no: WO71/509; p117, extract from the novel *Private Peaceful* copyright Michael Morpurgo 2003; p118, "The Deserter" by Gilbert Frankau appears in *The Poetical Works*, Chatto and Windus 1923, reprinted by permission of AP WATT Ltd; p124, "The General" by Siegfried Sassoon, copyright Siegfried Sassoon is reproduced by kind permission of George Sassoon.

Playscript copyright © Simon Reade 2006. Based on the novel *Private Peaceful* by Michael Morpurgo © Michael Morpurgo 2003

10 9 8 7 6 5 4 3 2

ISBN-13 978-0-00-722486-9
ISBN-10 0-00-722486-9

British Library Cataloguing in Publication Data

A Catalogue record for this publication is available from the British Library

For Paul Chequer and Alexander Campbell – SR

Contents

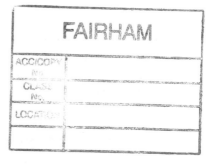

The Writers

Michael Morpurgo

Michael Morpurgo has been called "The Father of Children's Literature". His books have won many awards and have been translated into over 26 languages. *Private Peaceful* has won awards in Great Britain, France, Switzerland and the USA. For two years, 2003 – 2005, he held the post of Children's Laureate and travelled widely, taking his love of story to children in the Western Isles of Scotland, Wales, England, all over Europe and even to Moscow and Soweto in South Africa. In 1976 he and his wife Clare set up the charity Farms for City Children which now runs three farms welcoming over 3000 children a year.

Simon Reade

Simon Reade is Artistic Director of Bristol Old Vic where he has adapted and directed a one-man touring version of *Private Peaceful*. His other adaptations for Bristol Old Vic include *Alice's Adventures in Wonderland* (winner of the TMA Award for Best Show for Young People), Philip Pullman's *Aladdin and the Enchanted Lamp* and Jill Tomlinson's *The Owl Who Was Afraid Of The Dark*.

He was formerly Literary Manager and Dramaturg of the Royal Shakespeare Company where his adaptations included *Midnight's Children* (with Salman Rushdie and Tim Supple) and Ted Hughes' *Tales from Ovid* (with Tim Supple). For the RSC he also wrote the play *Epitaph for the Official Secrets Act* (with Paul Greengrass) and abridged Shaw's *Back to Methuselah* (with David Fielding).

Characters

In order of appearance:

DEVON:

TOMMO	Thomas Peaceful
CHARLIE	Tommo's older brother
MR MUNNINGS	the school master
MISS McALLISTER	Tommo's school teacher
MOLLY	Charlie and Tommo's friend
NIPPER	a Biggun at school, later on the Front Line
PETE	a Biggun at school, later on the Front Line
JAMES PEACEFUL	Tommo, Charlie and Big Joe's father
MOTHER	Tommo, Charlie and Big Joe's mother
BIG JOE	Tommo and Charlie's older brother
LES	a Tiddler at school, son of a rat catcher, later on the Front Line
GRANDMA WOLF	Mother's aunt
COLONEL	squire of Iddesleigh
JIMMY PARSONS	Charlie and Tommo's school enemy

MOLLY'S MOTHER

SERGEANT MAJOR

TOOTHLESS OLD LADY

RECRUITING SERGEANT

TIDDLERS

BIGGUNS

HATHERLEIGH MARKET CROWD

WAR:

SERGEANT 'HORRIBLE' HANLEY

BRIGADIER

WOUNDED SOLDIER

ORDERLY

CAPTAIN WILKES

ESTAMINET OWNER

ANNA – estaminet owner's daughter

INJURED GERMAN SOLDIER

LIEUTENANT BUCKLAND

GERMAN SOLDIER IN GAS MASK

GUARD – to Charlie

OFFICER – firing squad

SOLDIERS – from both sides

ESTAMINET STAFF

It may be appropriate to have more than one performer play Tommo.

Note on the play

From five past ten on the night of June 24th 1916 to six o'clock on the morning of the 25th, Tommo looks back on his life as a young boy growing up in rural Devon and on his recent experiences fighting in the trenches.

Scenes are given separate numbers for ease of rehearsing and should not necessarily be observed for moments of scene change. The Tommo scenes in Flanders, in the time-ticking-away present, can snap into the following scene in the past without pause and follow on without hesitation from the preceding scenes set in the past. Indeed, the play has many scenes which can flow from one to another so the simplest of designs is desirable with the maximum of stage 'business' suggested through mime. No set is required and only the bare minimum of props should be used: a school room does not require school desks, homes don't require real doors, trenches don't require trench walls, real rifles don't even need to be used. It may be that one single versatile item is useful for a whole host of things – like a fold-up camp bed.

The play is written in the tradition of story-telling theatre where a space, performers, a story is all that is needed. A sense of place can be created through inventiveness and imagination.

Simon Reade

Private Peaceful

ACT I
Scene 1

Flanders. World War I.

Tommo *is by a bed*

TOMMO	Five past ten. They've gone now, and I'm alone at last. I have the whole night ahead of me, and I won't waste a single moment of it. I shan't sleep it away. I won't dream it away either. I mustn't, because every moment of it will be far too precious.
	I want to try to remember everything, just as it was, just as it happened. I've had nearly eighteen years of yesterdays and tomorrows, and tonight I must remember as many of them as I can. I want tonight to be long, as long as my life.
	Tonight, more than any other night of my life, I want to feel alive.

Scene 2

Iddesleigh, Devon.

Charlie *is leading* **Tommo** *by the hand up the lane to school.* **Tommo** *feels uncomfortable in his collar and boots – his laces are undone. He's dragging his feet.*

CHARLIE   Come on, Tommo! School's not that bad, honest. *(teasing)* Mr Munnings may have a raging temper, and I wouldn't get on the wrong side of him when his hands start twitching for his cane, and make sure you keep out of Jimmy Parsons' way…but it's not all bad!

TOMMO   Big Joe doesn't have to go to school and I don't think that's fair at all!

CHARLIE   Big Joe is Big Joe.

TOMMO   *(protesting)* He's much older than me. He's even older than you, and he's never been to school. He's allowed to stay at home, sitting up in his tree singing *Oranges and Lemons* all day long. Big Joe is always happy, always laughing. I wish I could be happy like him. I wish I could be at home like him. I don't want to go, Charlie. I don't want to go to school!

Tommo *stamps his foot and stops –* **Charlie** *stops too.*

CHARLIE   Piggyback? (**Tommo** *hops up on* **Charlie's** *back and clings on tight, trying not to weep or whimper)* First day's the worst, Tommo. It's not so bad. Honest.

TOMMO   Whenever you say 'honest', Charlie, I know it's not true.

*School. The school bell rings – **Charlie** and **Tommo** have arrived – two*
*silent rows of children line up – **Tommo** with the **Tiddlers**; **Charlie***
*with the **Bigguns**. **Charlie** winks at **Tommo**; **Tommo** blinks back.*
*Then **Mr Munnings** appears, cracking his knuckles.*

MR MUNNINGS   *(pointing right at **Tommo**)* Aha! *(everyone turns*
                *to look at **Tommo**)* A new boy, a new boy to
                add to my trials and tribulations. Name, boy?

TOMMO   Tommo, Sir. Thomas Peaceful.

MR MUNNINGS   Was not one Peaceful enough? What have I
                done to deserve another one? First a Charlie
                Peaceful, and now a Thomas Peaceful. Is
                there no end to my woes? Understand this
                Thomas Peaceful, that here I am your lord
                and master. You do what I say when I say it.
                You do not cheat, you do not lie, you do not
                blaspheme. You do not come to school in
                bare feet. And your hands will be clean.
                These are my commandments. Do I make
                myself absolutely clear?

TOMMO   *(whispering)* Yes sir.

*Tommo and the **Tiddlers** file past **Mr Munnings** and the **Bigguns**,*
*their hands behind their backs – **Charlie** smiles at **Tommo** – Miss*
McAllister greets Tommo.

MISS MCALLISTER *(Scots, smiling)* Thomas, you will be sitting
                there, next to Molly. And your laces are
                undone. *(The **Tiddlers** titter – **Tommo** hangs his*
                head in shame as he takes his place, tearful)
                Crying won't do your laces up, you know.

TOMMO   I can't, Miss.

MISS MCALLISTER Can't is not a word we use in my class,
                Thomas Peaceful. We shall just have to teach
                you to tie your bootlaces. That's what we're

all here for, Thomas, to learn. That's why we come to school, don't we? You show him, Molly. Molly's the oldest in my class, Thomas, and my best pupil. She'll help you.

Miss McAllister calls the register as *Molly* kneels in front of *Tommo* and ties his bootlaces – he almost reaches out and touches her hair. As she finishes, *Molly* looks up at him and smiles.

TOMMO   *(to Molly)* At home we don't wear boots, except for church. Father always wore his great hobnail boots – the boots he died in.

Scene 3

Forest.

FATHER   *(to **Tommo**)* Off you go, you scallywag, you.
                  Enjoy yourself.

Father *starts chopping away at a tree trunk (mimed), grunting and
groaning at every stroke. **Tommo** looks up as if into branches above.*

TOMMO   *(to himself)* Look at the tree, swaying and
                  creaking when all the other trees are
                  standing still, silent.

Tommo *stands and stares upwards. There is the sound of the tree falling
– like a roar of thunder.*

FATHER   Tommo! Tommo! Run, Tommo!

Tommo *is rooted to the spot but **Father** pushes him out of the way just
in time – **Tommo** looks back to his **father**, who has fallen like a felled
tree. He's on his back, his head turned away from **Tommo**, finger
pointing at him, the soles of his hobnail boots prominent, his eyes open
but unseeing.*

TOMMO   *(shaking his father)* Father! Father!

*But **Father** doesn't stir.*

Scene 4

St James' Church, Iddesleigh.

Hymn music tells us we're in church (so we need no actual pews, no pulpits etc).

Mother, **Big Joe**, **Charlie** and **Tommo** *sitting at the front –* **Grandma Wolf**, *in her black bonnet, sitting beside them, scowling at them.*

Tommo *is distracted – his eyes flitting back and forth, from front to back, side to side.*

TOMMO	*(whispering to **Big Joe**)* Look, Joe: a swallow. It's Father trying to escape. He told us in his next life he'd like to be a bird, so he could fly free wherever he wanted...

*The **Colonel** gets up as if into the pulpit.*

COLONEL	*(hand clutching his jacket lapel)* James Peaceful was a good man, one of the best workers I have ever known, the salt of the earth, always cheerful as he went about his work. The Peaceful family have been employed in one capacity or another, by my family, for five generations. In all his thirty years as forester on my estate James Peaceful was never once late for work. He was a credit to his family and his village.

*The **Colonel** drones on.*

CHARLIE	*(whispering to **Mother**)* He's just like Father said: a silly old fart! A mad old duffer!
MOTHER	*(whispering, stifling a laugh)* Charlie! We're in church. It's the Colonel who pays the wages and owns the roof over our heads. So you all

show him respect. *(consoling **Big Joe**)*
Father's not really in his coffin, Big Joe – he's
up in heaven *(pointing upwards)* up there.
He's happy, happy as the birds.

*****Tommo** looks upwards in the same direction as **Big Joe**.*

BIG JOE   Swallow!

TOMMO   *(to himself)* He was trying to save me...if only
                       I had run, he wouldn't now be lying dead...
                       all I can think is that I have killed my own
                       father.

Scene 5

Flanders. **Tommo** *by the bed.*

TOMMO   Twenty to Eleven.

I don't want to eat. Stew, potatoes and biscuits. I usually like stew, but I've no appetite for it. I've been nibbling at this biscuit, but I don't want it either. Not now.

It's a good thing Grandma Wolf isn't here. She always hated us for leaving food on our plates. 'Waste not, want not,' she'd say. Well, I'm wasting this, Wolfwoman, whether you like it or not.

Scene 6

Home. **Charlie**, **Tommo**, **Big Joe** *at supper,* **Mother** *serving up great dollops of bread and butter pudding (mimed). She leaves the room*

TOMMO   *(disappointed)* Bread and butter pudding?

CHARLIE   *(catching* **Tommo's** *eye)* Mmm. My favourite!

They shuffle their helpings onto **Big Joe's** *plate –* **Big Joe** *grins.*

TOMMO   *(whispering)* Is there anything you won't eat, Big Joe?

CHARLIE   *(whispering to* **Tommo***)* I bet he'd even eat rabbit droppings.

TOMMO   No!

CHARLIE   Do you want the bet?

TOMMO   Go on then!

Charlie reaches under the table for a paper bag.

CHARLIE   Here, Big Joe: fancy a sweet? *(***Big Joe*** takes the bag and pops each rabbit dropping into his mouth, savouring every one of them. He then offers* **Tommo** *and* **Charlie** *one)* No, Big Joe, they're especially for you, a present.

TOMMO   Not for me thanks, I'm stuffed.

Big Joe *smiles.* **Mother** *enters –* **Big Joe** *offers her the paper bag.*

MOTHER   What's this? Charlie? *(***Charlie*** makes a run for it)* Charlie! Come back here this minute! *(she puts her finger into Big Joe's mouth and*

	scoops out the rabbit droppings – and hands him a mug of water) Now, Joe, drink up. And Charlie, Tommo: have a sweet to keep Joe company.
TOMMO	Mother!
MOTHER	You're going nowhere until you do. *(**Charlie** and **Tommo** reluctantly eat a rabbit dropping each)* Horrible, isn't it? Horrible food for horrible children. Don't you treat Big Joe like that ever again.

Scene 7

School. Playtime. **Charlie** *is playing with some* **Bigguns.** **Nipper** *and* **Pete** *are bickering.*

NIPPER	My Dad's the best. Much better than your Dad, Pete.
PETE	He may be bigger, Nipper, but that doesn't make him better.
NIPPER	Who says?
PETE	I do.

Tommo is playing with **Les***, the rat-catcher's son.*

LES	So what does your Dad do, Tommo?
TOMMO	My Dad's dead, Les.
LES	Oh. My Dad's a rat-catcher.
TOMMO	Like the Pied Piper of Hamlyn?
LES	Yes. Only he doesn't like children.

Tommo sees **Big Joe** *arriving at the edge of the playground and runs over to him.*

TOMMO	Hello Joe! What have you got there? (**Big Joe** *opens his cupped hands enough for* **Tommo** *to see)* A slowworm! That's lovely! Did you get it from Father's grave?

Big Joe *nods and wanders off humming* Oranges and Lemons, *gazing down in wonder at the slowworm.* **Tommo** *watches him go –* **Jimmy Parsons** *taps* **Tommo** *hard on the shoulder.*

JIMMY PARSONS	*(sneering)* Who's got a loony for a brother?
TOMMO	What did you say, Jimmy Parsons?
JIMMY PARSONS	Your brother's a loony, off his head, off his rocker, nuts, barmy.

Fight: **Tommo** *goes for him, fists flailing, screaming – but doesn't land a single punch.* **Jimmy** *hits* **Tommo** *full in the face and sends him sprawling. Then he puts the boot in, hard.* **Tommo** *curls up into a ball, but* **Jimmy** *kicks his back, legs, everywhere (this needs to be carefully and safely choreographed, not improvised!)*

Then **Charlie** *grabs* **Jimmy** *round the neck pulling him to the ground. They roll over and over, punching each other and blaspheming.*

The whole school gathers round to watch, egging them on.

TIDDLERS/BIGGUNS Charlie! Charlie! Jimmy! Jimmy!

Mr Munnings runs out.

MR MUNNINGS	*(roaring)* What on earth…?!

Mr Munnings pulls them apart, takes them by their collars and drags them both off. The playground is hushed.

Molly leads **Tommo** *by the hand and with her handkerchief gently dabs the blood from his nose, hands, knee.*

MOLLY	I like Big Joe. He's kind. I like people who are kind.
TOMMO	*(beaming)* And I like people who like Big Joe!

Off: the noise of six strokes of the cane.

JIMMY PARSONS	*(off)* Ow, sir! Ow, sir! Ow, sir!

Off: the noise of six more strokes of the cane – but no response from
Charlie *– **Tommo** beams proudly. **Charlie** emerges into the school yard,*
hitching up his trousers, grinning – everyone crowds round.

TIDDLERS/BIGGUNS Did it hurt, Charlie? *(etc.)*

CHARLIE   Jimmy Parsons won't do it again, Tommo.
                        (sniggers) I hit him where it hurts: in the
                        goolies. *(**Charlie** lifts **Tommo's** chin and peers at
                        his nose)* Are you all right, Tommo?

TOMMO   My nose hurts a bit.

CHARLIE   Well, so does my bum!

*Molly laughs. **Tommo** laughs. **Charlie** laughs. The whole school*
laughs.

21

Scene 8

Home.

Charlie, Tommo, and Big Joe eating tea with Mother. A knock at the door. Mother seems to know who it might be, and takes her time to prepare herself.

COLONEL	I want a word, Mrs Peaceful. I think you know what I've come for.
MOTHER	Children, finish your tea. The Colonel and I won't be a moment.

The Colonel and Mother stand aside out of earshot – the children strain to listen. The Colonel doesn't look Mother in the eye.

COLONEL	It may seem a little indelicate to broach the subject so soon after your late husband's sad and untimely death. But it's a question of the cottage. Strictly speaking, of course, Mrs Peaceful, you have no right to live here any more. You know well enough that this is a tied cottage, tied to your late husband's job on the estate. Now of course with him gone…
MOTHER	I know what you're saying, Colonel. You want us out.
COLONEL	Well, I wouldn't put it quite like that. It's not that I want you out, Mrs Peaceful, not if we can come to some other arrangement.
MOTHER	Arrangement? What arrangement?
COLONEL	Well, as it happens there's a position up at the house that might suit you. My wife's lady's maid has just given notice. As you know my wife is not a well woman. These

days she spends most of her life in a wheelchair. She needs constant care and attention seven days a week.

MOTHER (*protesting*) But I have my children. Who would look after my children?

Pause.

COLONEL The two boys are old enough to fend for themselves, I should have thought. And as for the other one, there is the lunatic asylum in Exeter. I'm sure I could see to it that a place be found for –

MOTHER (*interrupting, suppressing her fury, cold but calm*) I could never do that, Colonel. Never. But if I want to keep a roof over our heads, then I have to find some way I can come to work for you as your wife's maid. That's what you're telling me, isn't it

COLONEL I'd say you understand the position perfectly, Mrs Peaceful. I couldn't have put it better myself. I shall need your agreement within the week. Good day Mrs Peaceful. And once again my condolences.

*The **Colonel** leaves.*

CHARLIE (*under his breath*) I hate that man. (***Mother** comes back*) What will happen now, Mother?

MOTHER Well, we'll have to do as we're told. And my aunt can come and look after Big Joe and you.

CHARLIE/TOMMO Grandma Wolf?!

Big Joe howls, like a wolf.

MOTHER   *(stifling laughter)* She's your great aunt, not your grandma. Show more respect.

CHARLIE   But she's still a wolf.

Mother neither confirms nor denies.

Scene 9

Home.

Tea. **Grandma Wolf** *shows* **Charlie**, **Tommo** *and* **Big Joe** *that she is now in charge.*

GRANDMA WOLF   Tommo: wash your hands before eating. Charlie: is your hair done?

CHARLIE   *(his mouth full)* But why…

GRANDMA WOLF   And don't talk with your mouth full. Tommo – don't leave anything on your plate. Waste not, want not. *(talking to* **Big Joe** *as if he's stupid/mad/a baby)* Big Joe: who's a clever boy then? Did you like your supper? Let mummy wipe your mouth. *(**Big Joe** starts singing* Oranges and Lemons, **Grandma Wolf** *smacks him)* And stop that ghastly singing at the table, you stupid big baby. *(**Big Joe** starts to rock and talk to himself)*

You haven't been brought up properly, you Peaceful children. Your manners are terrible. You don't know right from wrong. Your Mother married beneath her, of course. I told her then and I've told her since, she could have done far better for herself. But did she listen? Oh no. She had to marry the first man to turn her head, and him nothing but a forester. She was meant for better things, a better class of person. We were shopkeepers – we ran a proper shop, I can tell you – made a tidy profit, too. In a big way of business, I'll have you know. But oh no, she wouldn't have it. Broke your grandfather's heart, she did. And now look what she's come to: a lady's maid, at her age. Trouble. Your mother's always been nothing but trouble from the day she was born.

And you boys: you're nothing but coarse and vulgar. Why can't you be more like Molly? Her parents are proper people. Her father is groom up at the Big House. God-fearing people who have brought their child up well, good and strict. That Molly is a good influence. She'll teach you some manners.

Now, bed, the lot of you.

Grandma Wolf leaves.

Scene 10

Charlie and Tommo go to bed.

TOMMO	What are we going to do, Charlie?
CHARLIE	Once upon a time there was a Colonel who was secretly in love with Grandma Wolf. Grandma Wolf's nephews knew this and wanted to get rid of her.
TOMMO	Charlie!
CHARLIE	So one day, the nephews went up to the Big House and pushed the Colonel's wife into the lake and drowned her, and so Mother came home and everything was just as it had been before.
TOMMO	But what happens to Grandma Wolf?
CHARLIE	The Colonel and Grandma Wolf get married and live unhappily ever after, but because they were so old they had lots of little monster children born already old and wrinkly with gappy teeth: the girls with moustaches like Grandma Wolf, the boys with whiskers like the Colonel.
TOMMO	You're a right Charlie, Charlie! Good night.

Scene 11

Home.

*A knock at the door. It's the **Colonel**. **Mother** and **Grandma Wolf** go to him. The children strain to listen but can hear nothing.*

TOMMO	What's up, Charlie?
CHARLIE	Shh! I don't know.

***Grandma Wolf** and **Mother** return.*

GRANDMA WOLF	*(grandly)* Your Mother will explain. I have to get up to the Big House right away. I've work to do.

***Grandma Wolf** departs.*

CHARLIE	Well?
MOTHER	It's very sad news. The Colonel's wife has passed away.
TOMMO	*(terrified)* Charlie!
CHARLIE	It's got nothing to do with me, honest!
MOTHER	*(bemused)* Of course not, Charlie. She was a frail old woman and she's given up her struggle, that's all.
TOMMO	Does that mean you haven't got a job any more?
MOTHER	Let me explain. You know some time ago your great aunt used to work as a housekeeper up at the Big House?
CHARLIE	And then she got kicked out by the Colonel's wife.

28

| MOTHER | She lost her job, yes. Well, now the Colonel's wife has passed away it seems the Colonel wants your great aunt back as live-in housekeeper. She'll be moving up to the Big House as soon as possible. |

Big Joe, Charlie and Tommo cheer.

| CHARLIE | What about the cottage? Is the mad old duffer putting us out then? |

Pause.

| MOTHER | The Colonel's wife liked me. She made him promise to look after me if ever anything happened to her. So he's keeping that promise. Say what you like about the Colonel, he's a man of his word. I've agreed I'll do all his linen for him and his sewing work. Most of it I can bring home. So we'll have some money coming in. We'll manage. Well, are you happy? We're staying put! |

They all cheer – Big Joe the loudest.

Scene 12

*The cheers develop into **Charlie** and **Molly** racing ahead of **Tommo**, leaping over (imaginary) high meadow grass, **Molly's** plaits whirling about her head, **Charlie** and **Molly** laughing. **Tommo** is left behind.*

TOMMO   *(whining)* Wait for me!

*Charlie and **Molly** stop – look at each other – **Molly** goes back to fetch **Tommo**.*

MOLLY   *(taking **Tommo** by the hand)* Keep up, Tommo!

They hare along and then stop, take off their shoes and socks, (miming) squelching in mud.

TOMMO   I love mud! The smell of it, the feel of it, the larking about in it.

MOLLY   Hey, Charlie: I dare you to take off your clothes!

Pause

*Charlie strips off his top – he probably wears a vest underneath. Pause. Then **Molly** does likewise.*

MOLLY   Let's jump in the river!

*Molly and **Charlie** run off shrieking. There is the sound of splashing. **Tommo** is amazed.*

TOMMO   Put your clothes back on you two!

CHARLIE   *(off)* Come on in, Tommo! The water's lovely!

*Tommo sulks while we hear **Molly** and **Charlie** continue to splash and giggle off.*

MOLLY   *(coming back on)* Come on, Tommo. *(she covers her eyes with her fingers)* I won't watch. *(she peeps through her fingers)* Promise!

*Pause. Then **Tommo** strips off his top like them and makes a dash for it – **Molly** follows – more splashing and giggling. **Tommo**, **Charlie** and **Molly** come back on.*

MOLLY   *(going off again)* I'm going to get dressed. No peeping!

***Charlie** and **Tommo** turn their backs, then look at each other, then turn slowly and watch **Molly** getting dressed off-stage. Then **Molly** dashes back on, fully dressed.*

MOLLY   I want to die – right here and now! *(**Charlie** and **Tommo** look at each other, confused)* I never want tomorrow to come because no tomorrow could ever be as good as today. I know! *(she (mimes) gathering some pebbles from the riverbed)* I'm going to tell our future. I've seen the gypsies do it.

She (mimes) shaking the pebbles around in her cupped hands, closes her eyes, then scatters them on to the muddy shore. She kneels over them.

MOLLY   *(slowly, seriously, 'reading' the stones)* They say we'll always be together, the three of us, for ever and ever. They say that as long as we stick together we'll be lucky and happy. *(now smiling)* And the stones never lie. So you're stuck with me.

They set off home – but hear the distant drone of an engine.

TOMMO	What's that noise?
MOLLY	Must be the Colonel's car.
CHARLIE	His Rolls Royce is the only car for miles around.
TOMMO	But it's not coming from the road – it's coming from the sky!

They all look up.

ALL	An aeroplane!

They wave.

ALL	Hello!

Their eyeline follows an imaginary plane coming in lower – the noise of cows scattering, ducks quacking and the plane landing – the goggled pilot enters, beckoning them over.

PILOT	*(shouting over the roar of the engine)* Better not switch off! *(laughing as he lifts his goggles)* Might never get the damned thing started again. Listen, the truth is I reckon I'm a bit lost. That church up there on the hill, is that Lapford church?
CHARLIE	*(shouting back)* No. That's Iddesleigh. St. James's.
PILOT	*(looking down at his map)* Iddesleigh? You sure?
ALL	*(shouting)* Yes!
PILOT	Whoops! Then I really was lost. Jolly good thing I stopped, wasn't it? Thanks for your

help. Better be off. *(lowering his goggles and smiling at them)* Here. You like humbugs? *(he hands them a bag of sweets)* Cheerio then. Stand well back. Here we go.

The **pilot** *exits. The children watch him go and we hear the plane taking off – the children throw themselves face down in the long grass as the sound of the plane flying overhead scares them – when they roll over the noise of the plane dies away.*

Silence. Then the sound of a skylark singing. They suck on their humbugs.

MOLLY	Was that real? Did it really happen?
CHARLIE	We've got our humbugs, so it must have been real, mustn't it?
MOLLY	Every time I eat humbugs from now on, I'm going to think of that yellow aeroplane, and the three of us, and how we are right now.
TOMMO	Me too.
CHARLIE	Me too.

Scene 13

*Flanders. **Tommo** by the bed.*

TOMMO

Ten to midnight.

I'm not sure I ever really believed in God, even in Sunday school. In church I'd gaze up at Jesus hanging on the cross in the stained-glass window, and feel sorry for him because I could see how cruel it was and how much it must be hurting him. I knew he was a good and kind man. But I never really understood why God, who was supposed to be his father, and almighty and powerful, would let them do that to him, would let him suffer so much. I believed then, as I believe now, that crossed fingers and Molly's stones are every bit as reliable or unreliable as praying to God.

But if there's no God, then there can be no heaven. Tonight I want very much to believe there's a heaven, that there is a new life after death as Father said; that death is not a full stop.

After my twelfth birthday, Charlie and Molly left school. I was alone, a Biggun in Mr Munnings' class. I hated him now more than I feared him. Charlie and Molly found work up at the Big House. Molly was under-parlour maid, and Charlie found work in the Colonel's hunt kennels. But soon after, Charlie had a serious run-in with the Colonel.

Scene 14

Home. **Tommo**, **Charlie**, **Big Joe**.

TOMMO	Charlie?
CHARLIE	What?
TOMMO	I'm in trouble. Mr Munnings confiscated my humbugs. I hate him. I hope he chokes on them.

Pause.

CHARLIE	*(whispering)* Tommo.
TOMMO	What?
CHARLIE	I'm in trouble.
TOMMO	What've you done?
CHARLIE	I'm in real trouble, but I had to do it. You know Bertha, that whitey-looking foxhound up at the Big House?
TOMMO	Yes.
CHARLIE	Well, she's always been my favourite. And then this afternoon the Colonel comes by the kennels and tells me he's going to have to shoot her because she's no good at hunting any more. So you know what I did, Tommo?
TOMMO	No.
CHARLIE	I stole her. I ran off with her, through the trees so no one would see us.
TOMMO	Where is she now? What've you done with her?

CHARLIE	Remember that old forester's shack Father used, up in Ford's Cleave Wood? I've put her in there for the night. I gave her some food. Molly pinched some meat for me from the kitchen. Bertha'll be all right up there. No one'll hear her, with a bit of luck anyway.
TOMMO	But what'll you do with her tomorrow? What if the Colonel finds out?
CHARLIE	He'll know. As soon as they find Bertha gone, the Colonel will know it was me. I won't tell him where she is. I don't care what he does, I won't tell him.

A loud and incessant knocking at the door. **Mother** *enters and lets the* **Colonel** *in.* **Charlie**, **Tommo** *and* **Big Joe** *stare at the* **Colonel**.

COLONEL	*(thin-lipped, pale with fury)* I think you know why I've come, Mrs Peaceful.
MOTHER	No, Colonel, I don't.
COLONEL	*(shouting, shaking his stick at* **Charlie***)* So the young devil hasn't told you. *(***Big Joe** *whimpers and clutches* **Mother's** *hand)* That boy of yours is a despicable thief. In my employ, in a position of trust, he steals one of my foxhounds. Don't deny it, boy. I know it was you. Where is she? Is she here? Is she?

Mother *looks at* **Charlie**.

CHARLIE	He was going to shoot her, Mother. I had to do it.
COLONEL	*(roaring)* You see! He admits it! He admits it!

Big Joe *is wailing now.*

MOTHER	So you took her in order to save her, Charlie, is that right?
CHARLIE	Yes, Mother.
MOTHER	Well, you shouldn't have done that, Charlie, should you?
CHARLIE	No, Mother.
MOTHER	Will you tell the Colonel where you've hidden her?
CHARLIE	No, Mother.

A moment.

MOTHER	I didn't think so. *(looking **Colonel** full in the face)* Colonel, am I right in thinking that if you were going to shoot this dog, presumably it was because she's no use to you any more – as a foxhound I mean?
COLONEL	Yes, but what I do with my own animals, or why I do it, is no business of yours, Mrs Peaceful. I don't have to explain myself to you.
MOTHER	*(softly)* Of course not, Colonel, but if you were going to shoot her anyway, then you wouldn't mind if I were to take her off your hands and look after her, would you?
COLONEL	*(snaps)* You can do what you like with the damned dog. You can bloody well eat her for all I care. But your son stole her from me and I will not let that go unpunished.
MOTHER	*(to **Big Joe**)* Big Joe: please fetch the money mug. *(**Big Joe** does so)* Here, Colonel *(offering a coin)*. Sixpence. I'm buying the dog off you

for sixpence, not a bad price for a useless dog. So now it's not stolen, is it?

*The **Colonel** is dumfounded and looks at the sixpence in his hand, to **Mother**, to **Charlie**. He puts the sixpence in his waistcoat pocket and then points his stick at **Charlie**.*

COLONEL   Very well, but you can consider yourself no longer in my employ.

*He goes out, angry. **Charlie** and **Tommo** whoop and yahoo. **Big Joe** sings* Oranges and Lemons.

MOTHER   I don't know what you've got to be so almightily pleased about. You do know you've just lost your job, Charlie?

CHARLIE   I don't care. He can stuff his stinking job. I'll find another. You put the silly old fart in his place good and proper. And we've got Bertha.

Scene 15

TOMMO (to audience) After a few weeks going round all the farms in the parish looking for work, Charlie found a job as dairyman and shepherd at Farmer Cox's place on the other side of the village. He would go off before dawn to do the milking and was back home late in the cold evenings.

Charlie would come home, hang up his coat on Father's peg and put his boots outside in the porch where Father's boots had always been and warm his feet in the bottom oven, just as Father had done. That was the first time in my life I was ever really jealous of Charlie. I wanted to put my feet in the oven, and to come home from proper work, to earn money like Charlie did. Most of all though I wanted us to be a threesome again, for everything to be just as it had been. But nothing stays the same.

When I did see Molly, and it was only on Sundays now, she was as kind to me as she'd always been, but too kind almost, more like a mother to me than a friend. Her hair was cut shorter now, the plaits were gone, and that changed the whole look of her. Molly wasn't a girl any more. Then suddenly Molly stopped coming round altogether – so Charlie sent me to her cottage with a letter.

Scene 16

Molly's cottage. **Tommo** *knocks (on front door), clutching letter.* **Molly's Mother** *appears.*

MOLLY'S MOTHER   *(face like thunder, yelling)* Go away! Just go away! Don't you understand? We don't want your kind here. We don't want you bothering our Molly. She doesn't want to see you.

She exits. **Tommo** *puts the letter in his pocket and walks away but then sees* **Molly** *waving frantically at him, pointing.* **Tommo** *runs towards where she's pointing.* **Molly** *soon follows and takes* **Tommo** *by the hand.*

MOLLY   *(crying)* The Colonel came to our cottage – I overheard it all – he told Father that Charlie Peaceful is a thief and he'd heard that he'd been seeing much more of me than was good for me, and if my parents had any sense they would put a stop to it.

So my father won't let me see Charlie any more. *(brushing away her tears)* He won't let me see any of you. I'm so miserable without you, Tommo. I hate it up at the Big House without Charlie, and I hate it at home too. Father'll strap me if I see Charlie. I think he means it too.

TOMMO   Why?

MOLLY   He says I'm wicked. Born in sin. Mother says he's only trying to save me from myself, so I won't go to Hell. He's always talking about Hell. I won't go to Hell, will I, Tommo? *(**Tommo** leans over and kisses her on the cheek – she throws her arms around his neck, sobbing as if her heart would break)* I so want to see Charlie. I miss him so much.

TOMMO	Oh, that reminds me: here's a letter from Charlie.

Tommo gives her the letter – she tears it open and reads it at once.

MOLLY	Tell him yes. Yes, I will.
TOMMO	*(intrigued, puzzled, jealous)* Just yes?
MOLLY	Yes. Same time, same place, tomorrow. I'll write a letter back and you can give it to Charlie. *(she gets up and pulls **Tommo** to his feet)* I love you, Tommo. I love you both. And Big Joe, and Bertha.

*She kisses **Tommo** quickly and then goes.*

TOMMO	*(to audience)* That was the first of dozens of letters I delivered from Charlie to Molly and from Molly to Charlie over the weeks and months that followed. All through my last year at school I was their go-between postman. I didn't mind that much, because it meant I got to see Molly often, which was all that really mattered to me. It was all done in great secrecy – Charlie insisted on that. He made me swear on the Holy Bible to tell no one, not even Mother. He made me cross my heart and hope to die.
	Molly and I would meet most evenings and exchange letters in the same place, down by the brook, both of us having made quite sure we were not followed. We'd sit and talk there for a few precious minutes, often with the rain dripping through the trees.

The sound of wind and rain roaring violently in trees.

TOMMO	The trees might come down on us!

Molly and *Tommo* *run and burrow into a (pretend) haystack where they shiver like frightened rabbits.*

MOLLY	Do you know what they're all talking about up at the Big House? All the talk these days is of war with Germany.
TOMMO	War?
MOLLY	Everyone thinks it will happen sooner rather than later. I've read all about it myself in the newspaper, so it must be true.
TOMMO	I didn't know you read a newspaper?
MOLLY	It's my job, every morning, to iron the Colonel's *Times* before I take it to him in his study. He insists his newspaper should be crisp and dry, so that the ink doesn't come off on his fingers while he's reading it. I'll admit I don't really understand what the war is all about, but some archduke – whatever that is – has been shot in a place called Sarajevo – wherever that is – and Germany and France are very angry with each other about it. They're gathering their armies to fight with each other and, if they do, then we'll be in it soon because we have to fight on the French side against the Germans.
TOMMO	Why?
MOLLY	I don't know. But the Colonel is in a terrible mood about it all. Everyone up at the Big House is much more frightened of his moods than they are about the war! Although he's as gentle as a lamb compared to the Wolfwoman –

TOMMO	Wolfwoman?!
MOLLY	Grandma Wolf – everyone calls her the Wolfwoman nowadays, not just us! Someone put salt in her tea instead of sugar and she swears it was on purpose – which it probably was! She's been ranting and raving about it ever since, telling everyone she'll find out who it was. Meanwhile she treats us all as if we're guilty.
TOMMO	Was it you?
MOLLY	*(smiling)* Maybe – and maybe not.

Scene 17

TOMMO   (to audience) Mother had it all arranged before
               I left school. I was to go and work with Charlie
               up at Farmer Cox's. I went up there mostly to
               look after the horses at first. For me it couldn't
               have been better. I was with Charlie again,
               working alongside him on the farm.

               Charlie and I had been haymaking with
               Farmer Cox, buzzards wheeling above us all
               day, swallows skimming the mown grass – as
               if Father was there watching over us. When
               we arrived home later than usual, dusty and
               hungry, Mother was sitting bolt upright in
               her chair and opposite her: Molly and her
               Mother.

*Home. **Tommo** and **Charlie** arrive. Mother sits upright in her chair,
sewing; **Molly** and her **Mother** sit opposite. Everyone, even **Big Joe**,
looks grimfaced.*

MOTHER   (setting her sewing aside) Tommo. Charlie.
               Molly's mother has been waiting for you,
               Charlie. She has something she wants to say
               to you.

***Molly's Mother** hands **Charlie** a packet of letters tied up in a blue ribbon.*

MOLLY'S MOTHER (as hard as stone) Yours, I believe. I found
               them. I've read them, every one of them. So
               has Molly's father. So we know, we know
               everything. Don't bother to deny it, Charlie
               Peaceful. The evidence is here, in these
               letters. Molly has been punished already, her
               father has seen to that. I've never read
               anything so wicked in all my life. Never. All
               that love talk. Disgusting. But you've been
               meeting her as well, haven't you?

Charlie looks across at Molly.

CHARLIE	Yes.
MOLLY'S MOTHER	*(quivering with rage)* There. Didn't I tell you, Mrs Peaceful?
MOTHER	I'm sorry. But you'll still have to tell me why it is they shouldn't be meeting. Charlie's seventeen now, and Molly sixteen. Old enough, I'd say. I'm sure we both had our little rendezvous here and there when we were their age.
MOLLY'S MOTHER	*(sneering superciliously)* You speak for yourself, Mrs Peaceful. Molly's father and I made it quite plain to both of them. We forbade them to have anything to do with each other. It's wickedness, Mrs Peaceful, pure wickedness. The Colonel has warned us, you know, about your son's wicked thieving ways. Oh yes, we know all about him.
MOTHER	Really? Tell me, do you always do what the Colonel says? Do you always think what the Colonel thinks? If he said the earth was flat, would you believe him?

Molly's Mother stands, full of righteous indignation.

MOLLY'S MOTHER	I haven't come here to argue. I have come to tell of your son's misdemeanours, to say that I won't have him leading our Molly into the ways of wickedness and sin. He must never see her again, do you hear? If he does, then the Colonel will know about it. I have no more to say. Come along, Molly.

She takes Molly's hand firmly in her own and sweeps out of the cottage.

A moment.

MOTHER   Well. I'll get your supper, boys, shall I?

Mother and ***Big Joe*** *exit.*

Silence.

CHARLIE   I know I should've told you, Tommo. Molly said I should tell you. But I didn't want to. I couldn't, that's all.

TOMMO   Why not?

Pause.

CHARLIE   Because I know, and she does too. That's why she wouldn't tell you herself.

TOMMO   Know what?

CHARLIE   When it was just letters, it didn't seem to matter so much. But later, after we began seeing each other...we didn't want to hide it from you, Tommo, honest. But we didn't want to hurt you either. You love her, don't you? *(pause)* Well, so do I, Tommo. So you'll understand why I'm going to go on seeing her. I'll find a way no matter what that old cow says. *(turning to **Tommo**)* Still friends?

TOMMO   *(mumbling, not meaning it)* Friends.

Scene 18

Flanders. **Tommo** *by his bed.*

Tommo Nearly five to one.

There's a sliver of moon out there, a new moon, a silver fingernail. I wonder if they're looking at it back home. Bertha used to howl at the moon, I remember. If I had a sixpence in my pocket, I'd turn it over and make a wish.

It's no good wishing for the moon, no good wishing for the impossible.

One afternoon, Bertha went missing. We went up into the woods, whistling, calling for her. And then we came to Father's old shack – and the grass beside it was soaked with blood. Behind the shack was Bertha, laid out on the grass, her tongue lolling. She'd been shot. Dead. We all knew who'd shot her. Big Joe was devastated.

Scene 19

*Iddesleigh – **Mother**, **Charlie**, **Tommo**.*

MOTHER   We don't have any choice. All that matters is that we find Big Joe. We need more people. I'll go up to the Big House right away to ask for the Colonel's help.

She exits. There is a hush.

TOMMO   I was just wondering… I was wondering where Big Joe would most want to be.

CHARLIE   What d'you mean?

TOMMO   Well, I think he'd want to be wherever Bertha is. So he'd want to be in Heaven, wouldn't he? So if he wanted to be with Bertha, then he'd have to go up to Heaven, wouldn't he?

CHARLIE   Are you saying Big Joe's killed himself to go up to Heaven and be with Bertha?!

TOMMO   No! Of course not! Listen: at Father's funeral, Mother told Big Joe that Father was up in Heaven. She was pointing upwards, I remember. I thought she was just pointing upwards in a general sort of a way, or at the swallow in the church maybe. But now I realise she was pointing to the top of the church, to the tower. It sounds silly, but I think Big Joe believes that Heaven is at the top of the church tower.

CHARLIE   Let's go! (***Charlie** and **Tommo** run but **Charlie** trips and twists his ankle*) You go, Tommo. I think I've done my ankle in. (***Tommo** proceeds*

*up the tower – a raised platform; or simply a
marked-out or specially-lit small square of the stage)*

Is he up there? Is he there?

*Tommo doesn't answer – he steps out on to the top of the tower and is
dazzled by sunlight – then he sees **Big Joe** curled up, thumb in mouth.
Tommo gently shakes him but **Big Joe** does not move.*

TOMMO   Wake up, Joe. For God's sake, wake up!

*Then **Big Joe** stirs.*

BIG JOE   Ha, Tommo. Ungwee. Ungwee.

TOMMO   *(shouting)* We've found him, Charlie. We've
                          got him. He's up here. He's all right.

Charlie punches the air and yahoos.

BIG JOE   Charlie! Charlie!

*The sound of the church bells ringing – which shocks **Big Joe** and
Tommo, but then **Tommo** laughs and **Big Joe** gives him a big hug –
and then starts singing Oranges and Lemons. **Tommo** joins in too.*

Scene 20

*Charlie, **Tommo** and **Big Joe** trot home.*

*Peacefuls' cottage. **Tommo** and **Charlie** enter with **Big Joe**.*

CHARLIE   Safe and sound!

*They see **Molly** sitting on floor with head on **Mother's** lap, her leather suitcase by their side.*

CHARLIE   What is it? What's happened now?

MOTHER   You may well ask, Charlie Peaceful. *(pause)* They've thrown her out, Charlie. Her mother and father have thrown her out, and it's your fault.

MOLLY   No! Don't say that. It isn't his fault. It's no one's fault.

*She runs over to **Charlie** and throws herself into his arms.*

CHARLIE   What's happened, Moll? What's going on?

***Molly** shakes her head and weeps. **Charlie** looks at **Mother**.*

MOTHER   What's going on, Charlie, is that she's going to have your baby.

Scene 21

TOMMO *(to audience)* They were married up in the church a short time later – a very empty church. There was no one there except the vicar and the five of us, and the vicar's wife sitting at the back. Everyone knew about Molly's baby by now, so the vicar agreed to marry them only on certain conditions: 'That no bells are rung, no hymns sung'. He rushed through the marriage service as if he wanted to be somewhere else. There was no wedding feast afterwards, just a cup of tea and some fruit-cake when we got home.

I moved into Big Joe's room and slept with him in his bed, which wasn't easy because Big Joe was big, and the bed very narrow. He talked loudly to himself in his dreams, and tossed and turned all night long. But, as I lay awake, what troubled me most was that in the next room slept the two people I most loved in all the world who, in finding each other, had deserted me. I thought of them lying in each other's arms and I wanted to hate them.

At home, I tried never to be alone with Molly – I didn't know what to say to her any more. I tried to avoid Charlie, too. On the farm, I took every opportunity that came my way to work on my own. Farmer Cox was always sending me off on some errand or other and I always took my time about it. It was while I was making a delivery to Hatherleigh Market one day that I came face to face with the war for the first time.

Hatherleigh Market. Bustle. A military band plays God Save the King. *Union Jack fluttering behind him, a Sergeant Major in scarlet uniform climbs up onto the steps, stick slipped smartly under his arm, and addresses the gathered crowd.*

SERGEANT MAJOR   *(rasping, commanding)* Ladies and gentlemen, boys and girls: I shan't beat about the bush. I shan't tell you it's all tickety-boo out there in France – there's been too much of that nonsense already in my view. I've been there. I've seen it for myself. So I'll tell you straight. It's no picnic. It's hard slog. Only one question to ask yourself about this war: who would you rather see marching through your streets: us lot, or the Hun? Because, mark my words, ladies and gentlemen, if we don't stop them out in France the Germans will be here, right here on your doorstep. They'll come marching through, burning your houses, killing your children, violating your women. They've beaten brave little Belgium, swallowed her up in one gulp. And now they've taken a fair slice of France too. Unless we beat them at their own game, they'll gobble us up as well. Well? Do you want the Hun here? Do you?

CROWD   No!

SERGEANT MAJOR   Shall we knock the stuffing out of them then?

CROWD   Yes!

SERGEANT MAJOR   *(nodding)* Good. Very good. Then we shall need you. *(he points his stick into the crowd, Kitchener-like, picking out the young men)* You, and you and you. *(pointing at **Tommo**)* And you too, my lad! Your King needs you. Your country needs you. And all the brave lads out in France need you too. *(smiling, fingering his moustache)* And remember one thing, lads –

and I can vouch for this – all the ladies love a soldier. *(the ladies in the crowd laugh and giggle)* So who'll be the first brave lad to come up and take the King's shilling? *(no one moves)* Who'll lead the way? I'm looking for boys with hearts of oak, lads who love their King and country, men who hate the lousy Hun.

*Jimmy Parsons steps forward, cheered by the crowd. Others follow. A toothless old lady prods **Tommo** in the small of his back.*

TOOTHLESS OLD LADY	*(croaking, pointing with her crooked finger)* Go on, son. You go and fight. It's every man's duty to fight when his country calls, that's what I say. Go on. Y'ain't a coward, are you? *(The crowd is looking at **Tommo**. The **Old Lady** jabs him again, pushing him forward)* Y'ain't a coward, are you? Y'ain't a coward? *(**Tommo** sidles away slowly, backing out of the crowd)* Chicken! Chicken!

Tommo runs helter-skelter down the High Street and away. Then he stops.

TOMMO	How fine and manly the men look in their bright uniforms. Maybe Molly will admire me – might even love me – if I join up and come home in my scarlet uniform? Mother would be proud. And Big Joe. I'll go to France and kick the stuffing out of those lousy Germans!

He runs all the way home.

Scene 22

*Cottage. The bustle of supper with **Tommo**, **Charlie**, **Molly**, **Big Joe**, **Mother**.*

TOMMO	Farmer Cox sent me to Hatherleigh Market this morning. The army was there, recruiting. Jimmy Parsons joined up. Lots of others too.
MOTHER	Don't worry about it, Tommo, they can't make you go. You're too young anyway.
TOMMO	I'm nearly sixteen.
CHARLIE	You've got to be seventeen. They don't want boys.
TOMMO	I'm not a boy!
MOLLY	They shouldn't take the men either. What are the women supposed to do, fend for themselves? What about the mothers? You wouldn't go Charlie, would you?

Pause.

CHARLIE	I'll be honest, Moll. It's been bothering me a lot just lately. I don't want to go. I'd shoot a rat because it might bite me. I'd shoot a rabbit because I can eat it. Why would I ever want to shoot a German? Never even met a German. But I've seen the lists in the papers – y'know, all the killed and the wounded. Pages of them. Poor beggars. It hardly seems right, does it, me being here, enjoying life, while they're over there. It's not all bad, Moll. I saw Benny Copplestone yesterday, sporting his uniform up at the pub. He's back on leave, been out in Belgium. He says we've

got the Germans on the run now. One big push, he reckons, and they'll all be running back to Berlin with their tails between their legs, and then all our boys can come home.

MOLLY   Oh Charlie, I don't want you to go.

CHARLIE   Don't worry, Moll. With a bit of luck I'll be back to wet the baby's head. And Tommo will look after you. He'll be the man about the place, won't you, Tommo?

TOMMO   I'm not staying. I'm coming with you, Charlie. I love what I know: and what I know is my family, and you, Molly, and the countryside I've grown up in. I don't want an enemy soldier ever setting foot on our soil. I'll do all I can to protect the people I love. And I will do it with you, Charlie. I have to prove myself. I have to prove myself to myself.

Interval.

ACT II
Scene 23

*Flanders. **Tommo** by the bed.*

TOMMO	Fourteen minutes past two.

I keep checking the time. I promised myself I wouldn't, but I can't seem to help myself. Each time I do it, I put the watch to my ear and listen for the tick. It's still there, softly slicing away the seconds, then the minutes, then the hours.

Charlie told me this watch would never stop, never let me down, unless I forgot to wind it. 'The best watch in the world,' he said, 'a wonderful watch!' But it isn't. If it was such a wonderful watch it would do more than simply keep the time – any old watch can do that. A truly wonderful watch would make time. Then, if it stopped, time itself would have to stand still, then this night would never have to end and morning would never come.

Charlie said we were living on borrowed time out here.

Scene 24

Training Camp. Salisbury Plain.

Drilling. Stood to attention.

SERGEANT HANLEY *(to Charlie)* Stand still! Stomach in, chest out, Look to your front, Peaceful, you horrible little man! Down in that mud, Peaceful, where you belong, you nasty little worm. Down! Are you the best they can send us these days, Peaceful? Vermin, that's what you are. Lousy vermin, and I've got to make a soldier of you. What's with this cap badge, Peaceful? It's crooked. You're a blot on Creation, Peaceful. What are you?

CHARLIE *(clear, firm, utterly without fear)* Happy to be here, Sergeant.

*From Devon, **Nipper**, **Les** and **Pete** join **Tommo** and **Charlie** and the other soldiers as they clump about like clowns in tin hats and khaki.*

NIPPER Hey, Tommo, look at you with your face like a baby's bum! You know what a razor is yet?

CHARLIE *(giving **Nipper** a little look)* Tommo and I are twins. Seventeen-year-old twins. Don't you forget it, Nipper.

SERGEANT HANLEY *(to Charlie)* Faster! You want to get your head blown off, Peaceful?

CHARLIE No, Sergeant!

SERGEANT HANLEY You want to get your arse blown off, Peaceful?

CHARLIE No, Sergeant!

SERGEANT HANLEY You want to get your nuts blown off,
                Peaceful?

CHARLIE   Certainly not, Sir!

PETE   I don't like what you're up to, Charlie. You're
                stirring 'Horrible' Hanley up unnecessarily.
                It's going to make things difficult for the rest
                of us.

CHARLIE   But that doesn't mean I have to lie down and
                let him walk all over me. I'll be all right.

(Drilling. Stood to attention. **Sergeant Hanley** *grabs* **Tommo's** *rifle and looks down the barrel)*

SERGEANT HANLEY *(to* **Tommo***)* Dirty. Five times at the double
                around the parade ground, holding your rifle
                above your head, Peaceful. *(after only two
                circuits,* **Tommo** *just can't keep his rifle up)* Every
                time you let that rifle fall, Peaceful, you begin
                the punishment again. Five more, Peaceful.

Tommo *begins again, head swimming, staggering.*

CHARLIE   Hanley!

Charlie *runs at* **Sergeant Hanley** *– they scream at each other nose to nose, simultaneously.*

SERGEANT HANLEY What do you think you're doing, Peaceful?
                Who do you think you are?

CHARLIE   How dare you treat my brother like that!
                You're a bully, Sergeant, that's what you are!

Charlie *is bundled off. Then the* **Brigadier** *enters, the recruits stand to attention.*

58

BRIGADIER   Let this be a warning to you all. Insubordination in a time of war could be seen as mutiny, and mutiny is punishable by death by firing squad. But this time Private Peaceful has got off lightly. Field Punishment Number One. Sergeant Hanley? *(**Sergeant Hanley** enters)* Punish the soldier, Sergeant.

SERGEANT HANLEY Yes, sir.

Scene 25

*Flanders. **Tommo** by the bed.*

TOMMO A minute past three.

I'm not asleep. I should be able to fight off sleep by now. I've done it often enough on lookout in the trenches. I long for that moment when you surrender to sleep, just drift away into the warmth of nothingness. After this night is over, I can drift away, I can sleep for ever.

Oranges and Lemons, say the bells of St. Clements,
You owe me five farthings, say the bells of St. Martins.
When will you pay me? say the bells of Old Bailey.
When I grow rich, say the bells of Shoreditch.
When will that be? say the bells of Stepney.
I'm sure I don't know, say the great bells at Bow.
Here comes a candle to light you to bed,
And here comes a chopper to chop off your head.
Chip, Chop, Chip, Chop, the last – man's –

They tell us we're going over to France, and we're all relieved. We're leaving Sergeant Hanley far behind us.

Scene 26

The blast of a ship's horn.

Quayside. As they disembark, the new soldiers see the walking wounded shuffling along, some with their eyes bandaged, holding on to the shoulder of the one in front, others on stretchers.

WOUNDED   G'luck lads. Give 'em what for.
SOLDIER

The sound of two aeroplanes buzzing overhead.

TOMMO   Which aeroplane's ours, Charlie?

CHARLIE   They're too far away... maybe it's the smaller one.

TOMMO   Come on small fellow! I wonder if the pilot from the yellow plane is up there? I can almost taste the humbugs.

CHARLIE   One of them's hit.

TOMMO   It's the smaller one...

Scene 27

Rest Camp.

ORDERLY	Letters. Letters for Private Peaceful.
CHARLIE	Which one?
ORDERLY	How many of you are there?
CHARLIE	There's me, Charlie, and my brother Tommo.
ORDERLY	You're in luck – there's one for you both.

He hands them the letters.

MOLLY   *(letter)* Dear Charlie and Tommo,

I hope you are both well. There's no escaping the war anywhere now it seems. They're turning most of the Big House into a hospital for officers, and the Wolfwoman rules the roost up there more than ever. She wears a lady's wide-brimmed straw hat with a big white ostrich feather instead of her old black bonnet, and she smiles all the time like Lady Muck.

I am missing you both. I am well although I feel a little bit sick sometimes. I hope the war will be over quickly and then we can all be together again. Take care of each other, now.

Your loving Molly.

CAPTAIN WILKES   Chop chop, everyone we're off to an estaminet.

TOMMO   A what?

CAPTAIN WILKES   An estaminet, a sort of pub.

Cheers all round.

Scene 28

Estaminet. **Pete**, **Nipper**, **Les**, **Charlie** *and* **Tommo** *drink themselves silly – a girl, clearing up, smiles at* **Tommo**.

NIPPER   Who's your friend, Tommo?

Tommo *blushes. The owner, who looks like Father Christmas without the beard, notices the smirks.*

ESTAMINET OWNER You keep your eyes to yourselves, boys, she's my daughter.

CHARLIE   *(raising his glass)* To Sergeant Hanley!

ALL   To Sergeant Hanley!

CHARLIE   And the Colonel!

TOMMO   The Colonel!

CHARLIE   And the Wolfwoman!

TOMMO   Wolfwoman!

CHARLIE   May they receive all the misfortune in the world and all the misery and all the little monster children they so richly deserve!

Scene 29

Camp. The next morning.

CAPTAIN WILKES   Men. Remember your training. Not a whisper, not a word. If the German gunners spot us, we're done for. Their front line is less than two hundred yards from our own. So, no smoking in the trenches at night, unless your want your head shot off.

PETE   Why's that, Captain?

CAPTAIN WILKES   Think about it, Pete: they'll spot the red glow of your cigarette tip, take aim, fire! Our trenches and our dugouts have been left in a mess by the previous occupants, so there's no brewing up this morning until we've cleared things up. *(collective groan)* Listen, I'm meticulous about tidiness and cleanliness in the trenches because of the rats. Let's get cracking.

Tommo is shoring up a dilapidated trench wall – he plunges his shovel in and opens up an entire nest of rats (all mimed).

TOMMO   Aghh! Rats!

LES   Stamp them to death.

Tommo tries to.

TOMMO   I haven't killed a single one.

LES   Don't worry Tommo, I'll see to them. It's just like being at home!

TOMMO   It's not just the rats that are a bother, Les. These lice are terrible. It's all very well being

	told to burn them off with a lighted cigarette end, but they get everywhere they can: the folds of your skin, the creases of your clothes. How I long for a bath to drown the lot of them.
LES	Rats, lice. What about the rain?
TOMMO	The unending, drenching rain. It's running like a stream along the bottom of the trench. It's such stinky, gooey mud – it seems it wants to hold us and suck us down and drown us. I haven't had dry feet since I've got here. I go to sleep wet. I wake up wet and the cold soaks through my sodden clothes into my aching bones.
CHARLIE	Hey stop complaining lads, it could be worse. We could be in Devon!

*They all smile at **Charlie**.*

CAPTAIN WILKES	Word has come down from Headquarters that we must send out patrols to find out what regiments have come into the line opposite us and in what strength – now, I know some of you will be wondering why we have to do this when there are spotter planes doing that almost every day… but these are our orders. Peaceful brothers, Nipper, Pete, Les, I want you to come with me. We have to bring back one prisoner for questioning. And there's a double rum ration to set us on our way. *(hurray! They drink the rum, put on their woollen hats and camouflage their faces)* Right-o men. Over we go.

They go up over the top.

Scene 30

No-man's-land. They crawl on their bellies, snaking their way forward.

CHARLIE   *(whispering)* Stay close, Tommo.

TOMMO   *(whispering, to **Charlie**)* I'm not frightened, I'm excited. It's like we're out poaching again, Charlie.

They can hear the Germans: talking, laughter, a gramophone. They continue across No-Man's-Land, and drop down into the German trench.

TOMMO   *(whispering)* It's much deeper than ours, Charlie.

CHARLIE   *(whispering)* Wider too, and more solidly constructed.

They grip their rifles (mimed) and, bent double, move along the trench.

TOMMO   *(whispering)* We're making too much noise. Why has no-one heard us? Where are their sentries, for God's sake?

*Ahead **Captain Wilkes** waves them on (with his revolver). A flickering of light comes from ahead – that's where the voices and music are coming from. The trench floods with light as a German soldier emerges, shrugging on his coat. He spots the English soldiers – both sides freeze – then the German shrieks, turns and blunders back. Gunfire, then **Nipper** throws a grenade (mimed) and there is a blast which throws the English soldiers against the trench wall. **Les** has been shot through the head, dead.*

CHARLIE   It's Les. He's been shot. He's dead.

CAPTAIN WILKES   Grab the prisoner. Let's go!

The Germans all lie dead – except one, blood spattered, shaking.
Captain Wilkes *throws a coat over him and* **Pete** *bundles him out, the German whimpering. They scrabble their way along the trench, up over the top, and run. Then a flare goes up, seeming to catch them in broad daylight. They all throw themselves to the floor as the German machine guns and rifles open fire.*

TOMMO
I must think of Molly. If I'm going to die, I want her to be my last thought – sorry, Father, for what I did, I didn't mean to do it!

The flare dies.

CAPTAIN WILKES On your feet!

They run off again and then another flare goes up – they dive into a crater as more intense gunfire and shelling starts, **Charlie**, **Tommo** *and the German soldier huddled together.*

GERMAN SOLDIER Du lieber Gott! Du lieber Gott!

TOMMO
(to **Charlie***)* 'Gott'. They call God by the same name.

Captain Wilkes *is lying injured on the edge of the crater.*

CHARLIE
Captain Wilkes!

Captain Wilkes *doesn't respond so* **Charlie** *goes up the slope and turns him over.*

CAPTAIN WILKES It's my legs. I can't seem to move my legs. I won't make it. I'm leaving it to you to get them all back, Peaceful, and the prisoner. Go on now.

CHARLIE
No sir. If one goes we all go. Isn't that right, lads?

*They make their way across No-man's-Land, **Charlie** carrying the*
***Captain** on his back all the way. The stretcher bearers come for the*
***Captain**.*

CAPTAIN WILKES   *(to **Charlie**)* Take my watch, Peaceful. You've
given me more time on this earth.

CHARLIE   *(admiring the watch)* It's wonderful, sir. Ruddy
wonderful.

*The **Captain** is stretchered off – the German is led away.*

GERMAN SOLDIER   Danke. Danke sehr.

NIPPER   Funny that. Seeing him so close to, you can
hardly tell the difference.

TOMMO   Poor old Les.

Scene 31

Flanders. **Tommo** *by the bed.*

TOMMO

Twenty-five past three.

Earlier they came and asked me if I wanted someone to stay with me through the night. I said no. I even sent the padre away. They asked me if there was anything else I wanted, anything they could do to help, and I said there was nothing. Now I long to have them all here. We could have sung songs. We could have had egg and chips. We could have drunk ourselves silly and I could be numb with it by now.

Scene 32

Rest Camp.

LIEUTENANT BUCKLAND	We're being sent up to Ypres, men.
CHARLIE	I think you mean 'Wipers', sir.

The soldiers chuckle.

LIEUTENANT BUCKLAND	*(nervous)* Yes. Into the Wipers salient itself. For months now Fritz has been pounding away at Wipers, trying to batter it into submission. Time and again they've nearly broken through into the town, but each time we've repelled them. If we give way then Wipers will be lost. Wipers must not be lost.

They march off.

NIPPER	Lieutenant Buckland didn't say why it mustn't be lost.
CHARLIE	The Lieutenant's doing his best, he's straight out from England.
NIPPER	He might be very properly spoken, but he knows even less about fighting this war than we do. He's just a young pipsqueak. He should go back to school.
TOMMO	It's true, he seems younger than any of us – even me.

They arrive at their new trenches.

PETE	What's that sickly-sweet stench?
NIPPER	It has to be more than mud and stagnant water.
LIEUTENANT BUCKLAND	We'll clear up here. *(to **Tommo**)* Private Peaceful: you're on stand-to. Keep your eyes peeled. Keep your wits about you.

Tommo peers over No-Man's-Land.

TOMMO	A blasted wasteland.
	No fields or trees, not a blade of grass –
	Simply a land of mud and craters.
	Unnatural humps are scattered beyond our wire.
	They are the unburied,
	Some in field-grey uniforms,
	Some in khaki.
	One lies in the wire with his arm stretched heavenwards, his hand pointing.
	There are birds up there, and they are singing.

*The bombardment starts. **Tommo** cowers, **Nipper** has got the shakes.*

PETE	*(above the din)* It's all right, Nipper, it's all right.

Tommo begins to cry.

CHARLIE	*(above the din)* It's all right, Tommo, it's all right.

TOMMO	(screaming) It's not all right, Charlie. Make it stop, make the earth still again, make it quiet. When it's over they'll be coming for us, we'll have to be ready for them, for the gas maybe, or the flame-thrower, or the grenades, or the bayonets. But I don't mind how they come. Let them come. I just want this to stop. I want it to be over!

It does stop.

LIEUTENANT BUCKLAND	Onto the firestep men! Bayonets fixed!
CHARLIE	You'll be all right, Tommo. You'll be fine. Just do what I do. Stay by me.

The firing starts all along the line.

LIEUTENANT BUCKLAND	We've got the Germans on the run! We've got them on the run!

Charlie *is not there.*

TOMMO	Charlie! Where's Charlie?

Silence.

CHARLIE	(from no-man's-land) Hey! Anyone there? It's me, Charlie Peaceful. D Company. I'm coming in. Don't shoot. (**Charlie** comes in under the wire – **Tommo** is stunned) Tommo. Give us a hand, will you? (**Tommo** grabs him and tumbles him into the trench) Am I glad to see you!
TOMMO	What happened? Where did you go?

CHARLIE	I chased after them but they shot me in the foot, can you believe it? Shot right through my boot. I'm bleeding like a pig.
TOMMO	Does it hurt?
CHARLIE	I can't feel a thing. Don't you worry, Tommo. I'll be as right as rain. It's my ticket home. Some nice, kind Mister Fritz has given me the best present he could, a ticket home to Blighty. I'll give them your best, Tommo. Pete'll keep an eye on you for me. You'll look after him, won't you Pete?
PETE	Of course, Charlie.
TOMMO	*(snaps)* I don't need looking after.
CHARLIE	And make sure he behaves, Pete. That girl in the estaminet… she'll eat him alive! Hey, Tommo. I'll be back before you know it. Promise.
TOMMO	You'll see Molly, then, and Mother?
CHARLIE	Just let them try and stop me. With a bit of luck I could get to see the baby. Less than a month to go now, Tommo, and I'll be a father. You'll be an uncle. Think of that.

Scene 33

Estaminet. **Tommo** *and* **Pete** *are drinking.*

TOMMO	I'm going to desert.
PETE	Hey, that's enough of that kind of talk.
TOMMO	I'm going after Charlie. I'll make my way to the Channel and find a boat. I'll get back somehow.
PETE	Don't be daft! You get shot for desertion.
TOMMO	Oh you wouldn't understand.

Tommo *makes to leave.*

PETE	Where are you going?
TOMMO	Back to camp.
PETE	Well, you watch yourself now.

Tommo *leaves – outside the girl from the Estaminet is carrying a crate of wine bottles.*

ANNA	Tommy? *(**Tommo** stops in his tracks)* You are ill? *(**Tommo** shakes his head. Some moments)* How old?
TOMMO	Sixteen.
ANNA	Like me. I have seen you before I think? *(**Tommo** nods)* My name is Anna.
TOMMO	Tommo.
ANNA	It's true then. Every English soldier is called Tommy.

TOMMO	I'm not Tommy, I'm Tommo.
ANNA	It's the same. But you are different, different from the others, I think. What do you do at home, when you are not being a soldier.
TOMMO	I work on a farm.
ANNA	With animals?
TOMMO	Yes. Horses. *(she kisses him on the cheek)* I should be going.
ANNA	Until next time, then.
TOMMO	Good bye.
ANNA	Au revoir.

Tommo goes back to rest camp singing at the top of his voice.

TOMMO	Orange and Lemons say the bells of St Clement's…
NIPPER	You won't be so ruddy happy, Tommo, when you hear what I've got to tell you.
TOMMO	What?
NIPPER	Our new sergeant. It's only Horrible-bleeding-Hanley.

Scene 34

*Flanders. **Tommo** by the bed.*

TOMMO   Nearly four o'clock.

There is the beginning of day in the night sky, not the pale light of dawn yet, but night is certainly losing its darkness.

Morning at home used to be walking with Charlie to school, wading through piles of autumn leaves and stamping on the ice in the puddles; or Charlie and Molly and me coming up through the woods after a night's poaching on the Colonel's river, and crouching down to watch a badger that didn't know we were there. Morning here has always been to wake with the same dread in the pit of my stomach, knowing that I will have to look death in the face again, that up to now it may have been someone else's death, like Les, but that today it could be mine, that this may be my last sunrise, my last day on earth.

All that is different about this morning is that I know whose death it is and how it will happen.

Scene 35

Trench.

SOLDIER   *(off)* Gas! Gas!

The cry is echoed all along the trench – they all try frantically to pull on their gas masks.

SERGEANT HANLEY Fix bayonets! Fix bayonets!

TOMMO   *(inside gas mask)* Christ! Christ!

SERGEANT HANLEY *(pulling on his own gas mask)* You're panicking in there, Peaceful. A gas mask is like God, son. It'll work bloody miracles for you, but you've got to believe in it.

Men start running, staggering, falling.

TOMMO   But I don't believe in it! I don't believe in miracles.

*But **Sergeant Hanley** hasn't heard*

NIPPER   Tommo! Tommo!

*Nipper grabs **Tommo** and they run together – **Nipper** without gas mask – he falls and dies.*

TOMMO   I have to breathe now! I can't run without breathing!

Tommo trips and falls – his gas mask slips off – he pulls it back on but he's coughing, retching, choking. He runs away from the gas. He's on his hands and knees, vomiting. He looks up. A German Soldier in a gas mask is aiming his rifle straight at him.

GERMAN SOLDIER   Go boy. Go. Tommy go.
IN A GAS MASK

Tommo scrabbles away.

Scene 36

Rest Camp.

PETE Tommo! I was so worried about you.

TOMMO Don't you worry about me. Poor old Nipper – he's gone, Pete.

PETE Poor old Nipper.

Silence.

TOMMO What happened to you?

PETE I kept running. I regrouped with some of the others. We counter-attacked – we drove the Germans back and retook our frontline trenches. But what's the point? All that bloodshed and death for what? No gains on either side. Back to square one.

TOMMO We're still here. We're alive.

PETE Yes. You're right. *(pause)* But so is Horrible-bleeding Hanley. There is some good news: letters. You've got two of them, you lucky devil.

*He hands **Tommo** two letters.*

MOTHER *(letter)* My dear Son,

I hope this letter finds you in good health. I have such good news to tell you. Last Monday, in the early morning, Molly gave birth to a little boy. You can imagine also our surprise and joy when I answered a knock on the door less than a week later to find your brother Charlie standing in the porch. He looks thinner than I remember him and much older too. He says that in spite of everything we read in the papers here you have been having a fine time together over in Belgium. Everyone I meet in the village asks how you are, even your great aunt. She was the first to come and see the baby. She said that although he was handsome she thought he had rather pointed ears, which is untrue of course, and upset Molly greatly.

Much has changed in the village, and none of it for the better. More of our young men go to join up all the time. There are scarcely enough men to work the land. Hedges go untrimmed and many fields lie fallow. Sad to say Fred and Margaret Parsons had news only last month that Jimmy will not be coming home. It seems he died of his wounds in France.

Charlie tells us that very soon there will be another big push and then the war will be won and over with. Come home safe and soon.

Your loving Mother.

PETE   (angry) So that's what we're having, is it? "A fine time." Why does he tell them that? Why doesn't he say what it's really like out here, what a hopeless bloody mess it all is, how there's good men, thousands of them, dying for nothing – for nothing! I'll tell them. Give me half a chance and I'll tell them. Saying things like that, Charlie should be ashamed of himself.

CHARLIE   (letter) Dear Private Peaceful,

I am home again as you can see, Tommo.

80

I am the proud father, and you are the proud uncle, of the finest looking little fellow you ever saw. Molly tells me he is even more handsome than his father, which I'm very sure is not true.

You should know that we have decided the little fellow will be called Tommo. Each time we say his name it makes me think you are here with us, as we all wish you were. Molly has said that she wants to write a few words also, so I shall end now. Chin up.

Your brother Charlie,

or the other Private Peaceful.

MOLLY   *(letter)* Dear Tommo,

I write to say that I have told little Tommo all about his brave uncle, about how one day when this dreadful war is over, we shall all be together again. He has your blue eyes, Charlie's dark hair and Big Joe's great grin. Because of all this I love him more than I can say.

Your Molly.

Scene 37

*Estaminet. **Pete** and **Tommo** are drinking. A different girl is serving.*

TOMMO	*(to the girl)* Where is Anna?

*The girl shrugs as if she doesn't understand. **Tommo** rises.*

PETE	Where are you off to now, Tommo?
TOMMO	To look for her. *(he goes outside and sees the Estaminet Owner)* Anna? Is Anna here?
ESTAMINET OWNER	No. Anna isn't here. Anna will never be here again. Anna is dead. You hear this, Tommy? You have come here and you fight your war in my place. Why? Tell me this. Why?
TOMMO	What happened?
ESTAMINET OWNER	What happened? I tell you what happened. Two days ago I send Anna to fetch the eggs. She is driving the cart home along the road and a shell comes, a big Boche shell. Only one, but one is enough. I bury her today. So if you want to see my Anna, Tommy, then go to the graveyard. Then you can go to Hell, all of you, British, German, French, you think I care? And you can take your war to Hell with you, they will like it there. Leave me alone, Tommy, leave me alone.

Scene 38

Trench.

CHARLIE   *(grinning)* Afternoon, Tommo. Afternoon all. ***(Sergeant Hanley** approaches, **Charlie** continues, chirpily)* What a nice surprise, Sergeant, I heard you'd joined us.

SERGEANT HANLEY   And I heard you'd been malingering, Peaceful. I don't like malingerers. I've got my eye on you, Peaceful. You're a troublemaker. I'm warning you, one step out of line…

CHARLIE   Don't you worry yourself, Sergeant. I'll be as good as gold. Cross my heart and hope to die. *(pause)* Nice weather we're having, Sergeant. It's raining in Blighty, you know. Cats and dogs.

***Sergeant Hanley** pushes past.*

TOMMO   So, Charlie, how was home? How's Molly? Mother? Big Joe? The baby?

CHARLIE   Didn't you get our letters?

TOMMO   Yes.

CHARLIE   Well there we are; you know it all.

TOMMO   But those were letters. I want to know all about it from you.

CHARLIE   There's not much to say.

TOMMO   Charlie!

CHARLIE   It's like we're living two separate lives in two separate worlds, Tommo, and I want to keep it that way. I never want the one to touch the other. I didn't want to bring Horrible Hanley and whizzbangs back home, did I? And for me it's the same the other way round. Home's home. Here's here. It's difficult to explain, but little Tommo and Molly, Mother and Big Joe, they don't belong in this hellhole of a place, do they? By talking about them I bring them here, and I don't want to do that. You understand, Tommo? Don't you?

*A shell whistles over and explodes, the blast throwing them all to the ground. The world above erupts. **Tommo** is curled into a ball.*

TOMMO   Stop! Stop! For God's sake stop!

***Charlie** tries to comfort him, folding himself around **Tommo**, singing* Oranges and Lemons *– **Tommo** joins in – the whole dugout joins in – and then the shelling stops and the whistle goes for them all to go out over the top – they all move forward as if in a trance and then the biggest explosion of all brings them all to the ground.*

Scene 39

*Flanders. **Tommo** by the bed.*

TOMMO

Five to five.

Sixty-five minutes to go. How shall I live them? Should I eat a hearty breakfast? I don't want it. Shall I scream and shout? What would be the point? Shall I pray? Why? What for? Who to?

No. They will do what they will do. Field Marshall Haig is God out here, and Haig has signed. Haig has confirmed the sentence. He has decreed that Private Peaceful will die, will be shot for cowardice in the face of the enemy at six o'clock on the morning of the twenty-fifth of June 1916.

The firing squad will be having their breakfast by now, sipping their tea, hating what they will have to do. No one has told me exactly where it will happen. I don't want it to be in some dark prison yard with grey walls all around. I want it to be where there is sky and clouds and trees, and birds.

Scene 40

No-Man's-Land. The muffled sound of machine-gun fire. **Tommo** *lies in the mud.*

CHARLIE	Hang on, Tommo. Hang on. We'll get you out. *(Tommo is dragged into the open air by Charlie and Pete)* Thought we'd lost you, Tommo. The same shell that buried you killed half a dozen of the others. You were lucky. Your head's a bit of a mess. You lie still, Tommo. You've lost a lot of blood.
PETE	All Hell's broken loose out there. We're going down like flies, Charlie. They've got us pinned down, machine guns on three sides. Stick your head out there and you're a dead man.
TOMMO	Where are we?
PETE	Middle of bloody No-Man's-Land, that's where, some old German dugout. Can't go forward, can't go back.
CHARLIE	Then we'd best stay put for a while, hadn't we?
SERGEANT HANLEY	Stay put? Stay put? You listen to me, Peaceful. I give the orders round here. When I say we go, we go. Do I make myself clear? *(pause)* Soon as I give the word, we make a dash for it, and I mean all of us. No stragglers, no malingerers – that means you, Peaceful. Our orders are to press home the attack and then hold our ground. Only fifty yards or so to the German trenches. We'll get there easy.
TOMMO	*(whispering to Charlie)* Charlie, I don't think I can make it. I don't think I can stand up.

CHARLIE	It's all right. Don't you worry, we'll stay together, no matter what.
SERGEANT HANLEY	Right. This is it. We're going out. Make sure you've all got a full magazine and one up the spout. Everyone ready? On your feet. Let's go. *(nobody moves)* What in Hell's name is the matter with you lot? On your feet, damn you! On your feet!

Pause.

CHARLIE	I think they're thinking what I'm thinking, Sergeant. You take us out there now and the German machine guns'll just mow us down. They've seen us go in here, and they'll be waiting for us to come out. They're not stupid. Maybe we should stay here and then go back after dark. No point in going out there and getting ourselves killed for nothing, is there, Sergeant?
SERGEANT HANLEY	Are you disobeying my order, Peaceful?
CHARLIE	No, I'm just letting you know what I think. What we all think.
SERGEANT HANLEY	And I'm telling you, Peaceful, that if you don't come with us when we go, it won't be field punishment again. It'll be a court martial for you. It'll be the firing squad. Do you hear me, Peaceful? Do you hear me?
CHARLIE	Yes, Sergeant. I hear you. But the thing is, Sergeant, even if I wanted to, I can't go with you because I'd have to leave Tommo behind, and I can't do that. As you can see, Sergeant, he's been wounded. He can hardly walk, let alone run. I'm not leaving him. I'll be staying with him. Don't you worry about

us, Sergeant, we'll make our way back later
when it gets dark. We'll be all right.

SERGEANT HANLEY You miserable little worm, Peaceful. I should
shoot you right where you are and save the
firing squad the trouble. You lot, on your
feet. I want you men out there. Make no
mistake, it's a court martial for anyone
who stays.

The men get unwillingly to their feet.

SERGEANT HANLEY Go! Go! Go!

They go over the top, **Pete** *last.*

PETE   You should come, Charlie. He means it. The
bastard means what he says, I promise you.

CHARLIE   I know he does. So do I. G'luck, Pete. Keep
your head down. *(**Pete** goes. Pause. Then the
death rattle of machine guns)* Poor beggars.
Poor beggars.

Pause.

TOMMO   Maybe the Sergeant won't come back.

CHARLIE   Let's hope. Let's hope. *(silence. **Tommo** drifts off
to sleep)* Tommo? Tommo? You awake?

TOMMO   *(stirring)* Yes.

CHARLIE   Listen Tommo, I've been thinking. If the
worst happens –

TOMMO   It's not going to happen.

88

CHARLIE	Just listen, Tommo, will you? I want you to promise me you'll look after things. You understand what I'm saying? You promise?
TOMMO	Yes.

Silence.

CHARLIE	You still love her, don't you? You still love Moll? *(silence)* Good. And there's something else I want you to look after too. *(he takes off the watch)* There you are, Tommo. It's a wonderful watch, this. Never stopped, not once. Don't lose it. *(pause)* Now you can go back to sleep again.

*A long moment. Then **Sergeant Hanley** appears, **Tommo** awakes.*

SERGEANT HANLEY Time to go.

*Charlie half drags **Tommo** across No-Man's-Land – the stretcher bearers come for him – **Sergeant Hanley** leads **Charlie** away.*

Scene 41

Camp. A guard. **Tommo** *approaches.*

GUARD   Twenty minutes. Sorry. Orders.

Tommo *goes to* **Charlie** *– he's lying on a bed, sits up and smiles at*
Tommo.

CHARLIE   I hoped you'd come, Tommo. I didn't think
                 they'd let you. How's your head? All mended?

TOMMO   Good as new.

They hug one another.

CHARLIE   I want no tears, Tommo. This is going to be
                 difficult enough without tears. Understand?
                 (Tommo nods) You'll tell Mother and Molly
                 how it really was, won't you, Tommo? It's all
                 I care about now. I don't want them thinking
                 I was a coward. I don't want that. I want
                 them to know the truth.

TOMMO   Didn't you tell the court martial?

CHARLIE   Course I did. I tried, I tried my very best.
                 They had their one witness, Sergeant Hanley,
                 and he was all they needed. It wasn't a trial,
                 Tommo. They'd made up their minds I was
                 guilty before they even sat down. I had three
                 of them, a brigadier and two captains looking
                 down their noses at me. I told them
                 everything, Tommo, just like it happened. I
                 had nothing to be ashamed of, did I? I wasn't
                 going to hide anything. So I told them yes, I
                 did disobey the sergeant's order because the
                 order was stupid, suicidal – we all knew it

was – and that anyway I had to stay behind to look after you. They knew a dozen or more got wiped out in the attack, that no one even got as far as the German wire. They knew I was right, but it made no difference.

TOMMO   What about witnesses? You should have had witnesses. I could have told them.

CHARLIE   I asked for you, Tommo, but they wouldn't accept you because you were my brother. I asked for Pete, but then they told me Pete was missing. So they heard it all from Sergeant Hanley, and they swallowed everything he told them, like it was gospel truth. I think there's a big push coming and they wanted to make an example of someone, Tommo. And I was the Charlie. *(laughs)* A right Charlie. Then of course there was my record as a troublemaker, 'a mutinous troublemaker' Hanley called me. It was all there on my record. So was my foot.

TOMMO   Your foot?

CHARLIE   All foot wounds are suspicious, they said. It could have been self-inflicted   it goes on all the time, they said. I could have done it myself just to get myself out of the trenches and back to Blighty.

TOMMO   But it wasn't like that.

CHARLIE   Course it wasn't. They believed what they wanted to believe.

TOMMO   Didn't you have anyone to speak up for you? Like an officer or someone?

CHARLIE   I didn't think I needed one. Just tell them the truth, Charlie, and you'll be all right. That's what I thought. How wrong could I be? I thought maybe a letter of good character from Captain Wilkes would help. I was sure they'd listen to him, him being an officer and one of them. But they said he'd died six months previously of his wounds.

The whole court martial took less than an hour, Tommo. That's all they gave me. One hour for a man's life. Not a lot, is it? And do you know what the brigadier said, Tommo? He said I was a worthless man. Worthless. And then he passed sentence.

Tommo. Look on the bright side. It's no more than we face every day in the trenches. It'll be over very quick. It's all over and done with, or it will be soon anyway.

We won't talk of Big Joe or Mother or Moll, because I'll cry if I do, and I promised myself I wouldn't.

You've still got the watch. Keep it ticking for me, and when the time comes, give it to Little Tommo, so he'll have something from me. I'd like that. You'll make him a good father, like Father was to us.

TOMMO	I have to tell you Charlie, I killed Father. If only I had run when he called to me when the tree was falling, he wouldn't have died. I should have told you years ago, but I didn't dare.
CHARLIE	I always knew that, Tommo. So did Mother. You talk in your sleep. It wasn't your fault. It was the tree that killed Father, Tommo, not you.
TOMMO	You're the best friend I've ever had, the best person I've ever known.

Charlie starts to hum Oranges and Lemons…

| CHARLIE | It's what I'll be singing in the morning. It won't be God Save the ruddy King or All Things bleeding Bright and Beautiful. It'll be *Oranges and Lemons* for Big Joe, for all of us. |

The Guard enters.

| GUARD | Your time's up. Sorry. |

Charlie is led out. Charlie begins to sing Oranges and Lemons, *off.*

| OFFICER | *(off)* Present! Ready! Aim! Fire! |

A volley of shots. Birdsong.

| TOMMO | *(to audience)* Tomorrow the regiment is marching up towards the Somme. It is late June, and they say there's soon going to be an almighty push and we're going to be part of it. We'll push them all the way to Berlin. I've heard that before. All I know is that I must survive. I have promises to keep. |

In the First World War, between 1914 and 1918, over 290 soldiers of the British and Commonwealth armies were executed by firing squad, some for desertion, some for cowardice, two for simply sleeping at their posts.

Many of these men were traumatised by shell shock. Court martials were brief, the accused often unrepresented.

To this day the injustice they suffered has never been officially recognised. The British Government continues to refuse to grant posthumous pardons.

Staging the play

REHEARSING THE PLAY

It will be important to identify each of the different locations before you start rehearsals. Begin by making a list of the scenes. Create a chart that shows which characters appear in each scene. This will help any actors who are playing more than one part. Include the location and characters who appear in each scene, as well as any props, sound or lighting effects you plan to use, remembering that if you keep everything very simple and use mime to suggest most of the props the transitions between the different scenes will be smoother and speedier.

Scene	Location	Characters	Lighting	Sound	Props
Scene 1	Flanders	Tommo	Night	Gunfire	Lantern
Scene 2	School yard	Charlie Tommo Mr. Munnings Miss McAllister Molly	Daylight	Children's voices	Class Register School Bell

It is important to look again at Simon Reade's 'Note on the play' on page 7. The play has not been written with the intention that each change of scene should involve a change of set. As he states, "a sense of place can be created through inventiveness and imagination".

Each scene has been given a different number so it will be easier to rehearse the play. In practice, there is no need to separate the scenes so that the Tommo scenes in Flanders, in the time-ticking-away present, can snap into the following scene in the past without pause – and follow on without hesitation from the preceding scenes set in the past.

Discussion

Before you make any decisions about staging the play, look carefully at the performance space and consider the following questions:

- Where will you place your audience in relation to the action?

- Tommo (as narrator) provides the links between many of the scenes. Where will you place him on stage so that he is easily heard and seen? He needs to be close to the other actors, but also able to observe and comment on the action and join in when necessary.

- How can you use your space to present the different short scenes in the play effectively?

- How might the use of different levels help to suggest the various locations – for example the Peaceful's cottage, the church tower, the countryside, the trenches?

- How will you help the audience to identify these different locations?

If necessary, simple props can be used to identify different areas. For example, Tommo (as the narrator) might be sitting downstage on a simple iron bed or a crate, with an oil lantern beside him. The Peaceful family home can be indicated by a wooden table and a few chairs. Several large sacks or bales of straw could suggest both the rural setting of Act I and later the trenches in Act II.

COSTUMES

Like the setting, any costume or make-up should be very simple. With a large cast it will be easier to suggest the various characters by using very basic costumes and adding items to indicate the various roles rather than trying to provide realistic costumes for everyone.

For example, the male characters could wear shirts and trousers, perhaps with braces, in Act 1. The Colonel might wear a tweed jacket. Arm bands and perhaps helmets could be added to indicate different ranks for the scenes in Flanders. The soldiers could try the effect of suggesting weapons in mime and movement, or it might be possible to use imitation rifles. Long skirts and blouses will be sufficient for the female characters. Mother and Grandma Wolf might wear shawls.

PROJECTIONS, LIGHTING AND SPECIAL EFFECTS

A wall (or large screen behind the acting area on which images can be projected) may help in establishing atmosphere as well as different locations. You might use a rural background for Act I and actual documentary images from the trenches in Act II.

Lighting will help to suggest time changes and locations, as well as highlighting particular areas of the stage. Bright lighting for the countryside scenes will contrast with the gloom of the battlefield. You might choose to use a smoke machine to indicate the gas attack or strobe lighting to suggest the effect of guns. It will be helpful to focus a spotlight on Tommo as the narrator.

If your lighting equipment is limited, one lighting plan for all the scenes will still be effective, as long as the actors' faces and the action on stage are clearly visible.

SOUND AND MUSIC

The sounds of the countryside in Act I and the relentless noise of the battlefield in Act II will help to create the different worlds that Tommo is describing. Music in Act I (e.g. wartime songs during the recruiting scene) may be effective in highlighting the mood you wish to create. Before the play begins you might use popular music of the period in the auditorium and display posters to help build the atmosphere.

Some scenes may require particular effects, for example the arrival of the plane in Act I. Make sure that whatever sound effects you use will not drown out the actors' voices.

Big Joe's favourite song is *Oranges and Lemons* and it is used several times during the play, each time in a different context and with a different effect.

> Oranges and Lemons, say the bells of St. Clements,
> You owe me five farthings, say the bells of St. Martins.
> When will you pay me? say the bells of Old Bailey.
> When I grow rich, say the bells of Shoreditch.
> When will that be? say the bells of Stepney.
> I'm sure I don't know, say the great bells at Bow.
> Here comes a candle to light you to bed,
> And here comes a chopper to chop off your head.
> Clip, Chop, Clip, Chop, the last – man's – dead.

Experiment with different ways of singing the song – by having one actor sing it alone, or asking all the cast to sing the song at the same time. This might be effective at the very end of the play.

The use of this nursery rhyme is particularly appropriate, as it commemorates the public executions that used to take place at Tyburn, near Marble Arch, in London, and Charlie sings it as he is led to his death at the end of the play. The sinister last three lines of *Oranges and Lemons* were added to the original rhyme, probably by children. The night before the execution the condemned person would be awoken by candle light – 'here comes the candle to light you to bed' – and by the ringing of the Execution Bell, a large hand bell.

Exploring the Play and its Themes

WORLD WAR 1 – BACKGROUND AND CONTEXT

In June 1914 the heir to the Austrian throne, Archduke Franz Ferdinand, was shot dead in Sarajevo and Serb nationalists were blamed. The assassination gave Austria the perfect excuse to attack and defeat Serbia and war was declared. Events escalated with frightening rapidity. Russia and France declared war on Austria. This gave Germany, an ally of Austria, the justification it needed to enter the conflict. Britain joined the war when German troops invaded neutral Belgium. Australia, Canada, New Zealand, India and South Africa rallied to the defence of Britain, and Japan declared war on Germany. By 1917 Italy and the United States had entered the war on the side of the Allies.

What had started as a limited conflict between Austria and Serbia eventually resulted in the deaths of 16 million people worldwide. Almost every family in Britain was affected by the loss or wounding of a relative or friend during the four years of war. The conflict was brought to an end in 1918.

The First World War had a huge effect on civilian life. Food rationing was introduced, and recruiting caused severe labour shortages. For the first time large numbers of women were employed in industry, transport, agriculture and commerce as well as nursing and driving ambulances at the Front.

1914	1915	1916	1917	1918
Germany invades neutral Belgium	Women take up men's jobs at home	Conscription introduced for men aged between 18 and 41	United States joins the war and assists the Allies	Germany launches major offensive on the Western Front
Britain declares war on Germany	They work as nurses and ambulance drivers in Flanders	A million men are killed in ten months	Tank, submarine and gas warfare intensifies	Allies launch successful counter-offensives at the Marne and Amiens
Japan joins the Allied forces		The Battle of the Somme. More than 400,000 casualties between July and November	The Battle of Passchendaele	
War spreads to the seas	Trench warfare continues on the Western Front		Royal family change their surname to Windsor to appear more British	Armistice signed on November 11, ending the war at 11am.
The Battle of the Marne				
The war that 'would be over by Christmas' drags on	London attacked from the air by German Zeppelins	The Battle of Jutland takes place at sea		In Britain, women over 30 succeed in gaining the vote.

EXPLORING CHARACTER

The action of the play switches constantly between Tommo, the narrator, who acts as a link between scenes, and the flashbacks to his childhood in Act I and his experiences in Flanders in Act II, culminating in the execution of his brother, Charlie. It may be appropriate to have more than one actor play Tommo. Much of the emotional impact of the play will depend on how he is portrayed.

If you are playing Big Joe, be careful not to make him a figure of fun. He should be a sympathetic character with his own perspective on the world. If you are playing any of the other parts, or perhaps representing more than one character, the challenge will be to find some reality in each character and move beyond stereotyped 'goodies' or 'baddies'. Your body language, as well as what you say, will help to define your character, particularly in the case of the Colonel, Grandma Wolf and Sergeant 'Horrible' Hanley.

1 Representation

Work in a group and make a list of the key characters in the play.

- Which of these characters is the most sympathetic?

- Which is the least sympathetic?

- Which character is most responsible for the fact that Charlie loses his life?

When you have decided, label each person in your group as one of the characters in the play. Present your conclusions to each of these questions to the rest of the class by arranging your group with the most sympathetic at one end of the line and the least sympathetic at the other end. You could do the same for the question of who is responsible for Charlie's death, and for any other questions you come up with. Be prepared to justify your decisions to the rest of the class, who may have come to different conclusions.

2 Movement

The group walks slowly around the room. Take turns to call out the name of one of the characters in the play – the Colonel, Charlie, Grandma Wolf, Sergeant Hanley etc. Everyone immediately takes on the physical characteristics of that person. The aim is to try to indicate age, status and gender without caricaturing the person. Continue until all the major characters in the play have been included.

3 Writing Character Sketches

A novelist has the space to describe his characters, but in a play we learn what characters are like through their behaviour and through what other the characters say about them.

- Choose two contrasting characters from the play – perhaps a sympathetic person like Mother, and an unsympathetic one like the Colonel.

- Create two columns under each character's name. Head one of the columns POSITIVE and the other NEGATIVE.

- Find three or four adjectives to describe this person and decide in which column these should appear.

- Based on your lists, write a short character sketch of both characters.

- If you are able to visualize their appearance, add your ideas to this description.

- Compare your description with another person who has chosen the same character.

6. Discussion

Throughout the play, Charlie stands up to different authority figures and bullies. It is this aspect of his personality that leads him into trouble. Make a list of all the scenes where this occurs.

- Is he always right to oppose those he sees as bullies?

- How does his behaviour affect those around him, particularly Molly and Tommo?

- How far is he himself responsible for what happens to him in Flanders?

- Does he deserve his fate?

IN THE TRENCHES

A shallow trench on the Western Front in 1916.

Memories of World War I are dominated by images of the fearful loss of life in the battles of the Somme and Passchendaele. The futile frontal attacks with rifles and pistols against machine guns in the mud of Flanders and the unpopularity of General Haig and his staff officers led to the belief that the ordinary British soldiers were "lions led by donkeys".

At first, there was no conscription. Young men were encouraged to join up, and many believed that the war would be over in a matter of months. Those who did not want to join the army could be targeted by people as cowards – being handed white feathers and refused service in shops and pubs. But soon the government could not cover up the fact that many thousands of men had been killed or severely wounded. Sending wounded soldiers home late at night to London railway stations did not hide the fact that casualties were horrendous.

If ever I get sent to the Front with a regiment I shall almost shed tears of joy.

In 1914, Captain Noel Chavasse, was a young army doctor. These extracts from his letters reveal how his optimism and eagerness was soon changed by the terrible conditions in the trenches

Our men have had a terrible experience of 72 hours in trenches, drenched through and in some places knee-deep in mud and water. They don't look like strong young men. They are muddied to the eyes. Their coats are an awful weight with the water which has soaked in. Their backs are bent, and they stagger and totter along with the weight of their packs. Their faces are white and haggard and their eyes glare out from mud which with short, bristly beards give them an almost beastlike look. They look like wounded or sick wild things. I have seen nothing like it.

Poor jaded and terrified boys of 18 years of age are shot for shirking the cruel hardships of winter trenches – it fills us with dismay and rage. Why should trench-exhausted men be driven to collapse?

I have now had 4 stretcher bearers killed and one wounded, and one has had to go home with a strained heart and another because his nerves gave way after a very bad shelling. That is 7 out of 16 already.

We all hate the war worse than we thought we could.

In June 2005 Henry Allingham, a survivor of the war, reached the age of 109. He was Britain's oldest man. Even 90 years later he was haunted by the conditions in the trenches, the smell of gas, the bodies floating in the water, the lack of sanitation, as well as the moment he fell into a crumbling shell hole full of rats, bodies, arms and legs.

> "The water in the trenches through which we waded was alive with a multitude of swimming frogs. Red slugs crawled up the side of the trenches and strange beetles with dangerous looking horns wriggled along dry ledges and invaded the dugouts, in search of the lice that infested them."

"I MUST SURVIVE. I HAVE PROMISES TO KEEP."

At the end of the play, Tommo learns that his regiment has been ordered towards the river Somme. General Haig's tactics during the Battle of the Somme led to futile and indiscriminate slaughter. As the British divisions walked towards the German lines, they were mown down by machine guns. By the end of the first day, the British had suffered 60,000 casualties, of whom 20,000 were dead, the largest single loss. Sixty per cent of all officers were killed. Far from being a decisive victory, the battle ended in November with a gain of only five miles. In the play we are not told whether Tommo survives the war unhurt and returns to England to keep his promises. What do you think?

Drama Activity

1   Working in a small group, create a scene in which Tommo has returned home.

- Decide whether he has been wounded or if the war is over and he has returned physically unharmed.

- Choose the timing of your scene – either in the first few days after his return, or some time later when the changes caused by the war to Tommo and the family are becoming clear.

- Is everyone in the family – Big Joe, Molly, Mother and Charlie's son, little Tommo – still the same as they were before the brothers marched away?

2   If you decide that Tommo does not survive, create a scene showing the lives of the Peaceful family after the war.

- Again, choose the timing of the scene. If the deaths of Charlie and Tommo are recent, how will the family behave? What are their memories of the brothers? Do they know the truth about Charlie's death?

- If you decide to show the family at a later time, how will the double loss have affected each of them? Are they bitter about the way the war has changed their lives?

- If they are in financial difficulties, what decisions have they made? How have their relatives and neighbours reacted to their changed circumstances?

BOY SOLDIERS IN THE TRENCHES

When William Roberts was a 15-year-old schoolboy he learned of his father's death at the Battle of the Somme and decided to enlist. He was one of almost 40,000 recruits who were below the official enlistment age of 18. Some boys joined up out of a sense of patriotic duty but for others it was an escape from boring, badly paid work on farms and in factories, or from grinding poverty.

> *"I was 16 and working as a sales assistant… I earned 6 bob a week, and worked from 7 am to 7 pm six days a week. I gave most of the money to my mother. I hated being at home…When the recruiting sergeants and the bands came round it seemed like the most interesting thing that ever happened"*
>
> Clarrie Jarman

Private Reginald Giles of the First Battalion of the Gloucester Regiment died during the Battle of the Somme. Reginald shouldn't have been there at all. He was only fourteen. Like the thousands of other soldiers, he experienced the boredom and terror of trench warfare, the incessant pounding of artillery, the damp, lice-infested conditions, the stench of death and the screams of the wounded hanging on the barbed wire in No-Man's Land.

Recruiting Sergeants seldom enforced the minimum age requirement or asked young recruits to prove their age. Sixteen-year-old George Coppard tried to enlist.

> *"The sergeant said 'Clear off son. Come back tomorrow and see if you're nineteen, eh?' So I turned up again the next day and gave my age as nineteen. Holding up my right hand I swore to fight for King and Country. The sergeant winked as he gave me the King's shilling"*

Eva Dobell was a British nurse who worked in many hospitals during the war. She wrote poems about some of her patients.

Pluck

Crippled for life at seventeen,
His great eyes seems to question why:
With both legs smashed it might have been
Better in that grim trench to die
Than drag maimed years out helplessly.

A child – so wasted and so white,
He told a lie to get his way,
To march, a man with men, and fight
While other boys are still at play.
A gallant lie your heart will say.

So broke with pain, he shrinks in dread
To see the 'dresser' drawing near;
And winds the clothes about his head
That none may see his heart-sick fear.
His shaking, strangled sobs you hear.

But when the dreaded moment's there
He'll face us all, a soldier yet,
Watch his bared wounds with unmoved air,
(Though tell-tale lashes still are wet),
And smoke his Woodbine cigarette.

Eva Dobell

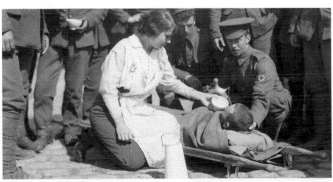

A nurse from the Medical Corps tends to a wounded soldier.

THE FIRING SQUAD

Like many other under-age recruits, Victor Sylvester ran away from school to enlist at the outbreak of the war. He was fighting on the Western Front at fifteen. As well as suffering the hardships of war in the trenches, Victor was ordered to take part in an execution.

> "The victim was brought out from a shed and led struggling to a chair to which he was then bound and a white handkerchief was placed over his heart as our target area. He was said to have fled in the face of the enemy. The tears were rolling down my cheeks as he tried to free himself from the ropes. I aimed blindly and when the gunsmoke had cleared away we were horrified to see that although wounded, the man was still alive. Still blindfolded, he was attempting to make a run for it still strapped to the chair, an officer in charge stepped forward to put the finishing touch with a revolver held to the poor man's temple. He had only once cried out and that was when he shouted the one word, 'mother'. He could not have been much older than me."

During Victor's time in Flanders he was ordered to take part in four further executions and the memory haunted him for the rest of his life.

In Lichfield, Staffordshire, there is the Shot At Dawn memorial in memory of servicemen executed for desertion or cowardice.

Drama

Organisation: Work in pairs. One of you is Victor, the other is an officer, or a sergeant major.

Situation: Victor has just heard that he has been ordered to join the firing squad for another execution. He tries to explain that he is very unhappy with this task. What arguments will he use? How will the officer or sergeant respond?

First line: What do you want, Private Sylvester?

Victor's parents suspected he had joined the army and informed the authorities in 1914 but it was not until he was wounded in 1917 that he was discovered and brought home to England. After the war he became a very successful dance band leader.

Drama

Organisation: Work in a group of three or four. One of you takes on the role of Victor. The others are his parents and perhaps another family member.

Situation: Victor is in hospital in England where his family visit him. Will he be able to tell them why he joined up, and what his experiences in the war were like?

First Line: Why didn't you write to us? We thought you were dead.

THE EXECUTION OF PRIVATE HARRY FARR

I certify that Private Harry Farr of First Battalion West Yorkshire regiment was executed by shooting at 6am on 18th October 1916. Death was instantaneous.

A. Anderson, Captain R.A.M.C.

306 British and Commonwealth soldiers were shot for cowardice and desertion during the First World War. Field Marshal Douglas Haig claimed that all soldiers charged with desertion or cowardice were medically examined and that no soldier was sentenced to death if suspected of suffering from shell-shock. Yet in the summer of 1916 a secret order was given instructing that cases of cowardice were always to be punished with death and medical excuses were not to be tolerated.

25 year-old Harry Farr had endured almost two years of trench warfare. Like many others, he developed a medical condition that was known as shell-shock. On four occasions during 1915–16 he reported sick with his nerves. In May 1915, he was in hospital for five months and had such an uncontrollable shake that nurses had to write his letters home to his wife. During April 1916 he reported sick again with his nerves and spent two weeks at a dressing station. In July 1916 he was in hospital for two days. During September he reported sick to Regimental Sergeant Major Haking who told him to go to the dressing station, but because he did not appear to be wounded he was refused treatment. Farr's court martial lasted about 20 minutes and most of the evidence was supplied by RMS Haking. There is no evidence that he was ever given an opportunity to request a "soldier's friend" – an officer to present his case – and so he defended himself.

Court Martial

Read the following extract from the transcript of Harry Farr's court martial, which is on file at the Public Record Office, File No: WO71/509. The complete transcript (and much more) is to be found on the website www.shotatdawn.org.uk

Field General Court Martial – VILLE-SUR-ANCRE, 2 October 1916

Alleged Offender: No.8871 Private Harry T. FARR, 1st Battalion West Yorkshire Regiment. Offence Charged: Section 4 (7) Army Act:

Misbehaving before the enemy in such a manner as to show cowardice

Plea: **Not Guilty**

Private Harry Farr. Sworn statement:

On 16th Sept. 1916 when going up to the trenches with my
Company I fell out sick. I could not find the Commanding
Officer to obtain permission. The Sergeant Major told me to go
to the advanced dressing station – but they would not see me
there as I was not wounded. The Sergeant Major told me to go
up with the ration party at night. I started with this party
and had to fall out sick – I could not get permission as I was
in the rear and the Sergeant Major was in front, but left word
with a Private soldier. I returned to the 1st Line Transport.
On the Sgt. Major's return I reported to him and said I was
sick and could not stand it. He said, "You are a damn coward
& you will go to the trenches. I don't give a damn for my life
& I don't give a damn for yours and I'll get you damn well
shot". I said to the Sergeant Major "You have got this all
made up for me".

The Sergeant Major told two men to take me up to the
trenches. They commenced to shove me – I told them not to as
I was sick enough as it was. The Sergeant Major grabbed my
rifle and said, "I'll blow your brains out if you don't go". I
called out for an officer but there were none there. I was then
tripped up & commenced to struggle. After this I found myself
back in the 1st Line Transport under a guard. If the escort
had not started to shove me about I would have gone up to
the Trenches: it was on account of their doing this that I
commenced to struggle.

1st Witness – No.7284 Regimental Sergeant Major H. HAKING,
1st Battalion West Yorkshire Regiment. Sworn statement:

The accused reported to me at the 1st Line Transport – he
stated he was sick and he could not find his Company
Commander for permission to fall out. I ordered him to report
sick at the Dressing Station but they would not see him as he

was not wounded. I then ordered him to join the ration party. On arrival at the ration dump Corporal Booth reported to me that the accused was missing. On returning I saw the accused standing near a brazier. I asked him why he was there. He replied "I cannot stand it, I cannot stand it". I ordered Corporal Booth to take him up to the trenches under escort. The accused commenced to scream and struggle. I warned him that he would have to go to the trenches or be tried for cowardice. He replied "I am not fit to go to the trenches". The accused again started struggling and screaming. I placed him in charge of a Guard.

2nd Witness – 2nd Lieutnant. L. P. Marshall West Yorkshire Regiment.

I have known the accused for the last 6 weeks. On working parties he has three times asked for leave to fall out & return to camp as he could not stand the noise of the artillery. He was trembling & did not appear in a fit state.

3rd Witness – Sergeant. J. Andrews, West Yorkshire Regiment.

The accused reported sick with nerves in April 1916 – the medical officer detained him for a fortnight in the dressing station. He reported again for the same cause on 22.7.16 and was detained for the day, being discharged to duty the following day. The medical officer, Captain Evans who examined him has been wounded and is not available to give evidence.

To: the Adjutant, 1st 7/10/16, W.Williams Medical Officer.

I hereby certify that I examined No.8871 Pte. H. Farr on Oct. 2nd 1916 and that in my opinion his general physical and mental condition were ~~good~~ satisfactory.

Report on 8871 Pte. Farr, H. 7.10.16, A Wilson, Capt. A Company

The present Commanding Officer is new and does not know the man's previous record. This man came out in November 1914 and was sent down to the Base with shell shock in May 1915. I cannot say what has destroyed this man's nerves, but he has proved himself on many occasions incapable of keeping his head in action & likely to cause a panic.

Apart from his behaviour under fire, his conduct & character are very good.

14th Corps. 4/10/16, C. Ross Maj. Gen Commander. 6th Division.

I recommend that the extreme penalty be enforced.

14th Corps, 4th Army. 6.10.16, Lieutenant General Cavan, Commanding 14th Corps

The charge of "cowardice" seems to be clearly proved and the Sergeant Major's opinion of the man is definitely bad to say the least of it. The G.O.C. 6th Div. informs me that the men know the man is no good.

I therefore recommend that the sentence be carried out.

General Headquarters, 11/10/1916
General Rawlinson, Commander, Fourth Army

I recommend that the sentence be carried out.

Finding and sentence: Guilty. Death.

Discussion

- Notice the similarities and differences between The Sergeant Major's account of what happened, and how Harry Farr describes the events leading to his arrest for cowardice. Which account seems the most truthful?

- What state of mind do you think the Sergeant Major might have been in?

- Do you think that the Sergeant Major acted fairly, under the circumstances?

- Farr claims that he said to the Sergeant Major "You have got this all made up for me". What do you think he meant by this?

- Why do you think that the Medical Officer changes his description of Farr's mental and physical state from 'good' to 'satisfactory'?

- Do you consider that Farr's behaviour showed cowardice?

Harry Farr has no known grave. The Army Chaplain, who attended his execution, sent a message of condolence via the local vicar to Farr's widow in which he said that a finer soldier never lived. He also revealed that Farr refused to be blindfolded when shot.

Harry's widow Gertrude was told at first that her husband had died in action. Later, when her pension was stopped, she learned that he had been shot for cowardice and she was not entitled to it. She hid the letter and was unable to tell her family for many years. "I didn't want anybody to know, not even my dear mother. It was a terrible thing – the stigma." Eventually she told Harry's parents the truth. His father was a staunch army man and as soon as he was told the window blinds were drawn in shame. When Gertrude was unable to pay her rent the landlord turned her out onto the streets with a small baby. Later she found work in domestic service. Each Armistice Day she felt a deep inner pain. "Nobody knows the feelings," she said, "Every year I feel worse because I look at all those men who've been through it and came home and think, my husband should be with them."

Drama

Organisation: Work with a partner. One of you takes on the role of Harry Farr and the other is Charlie Peaceful.

Situation: You are both in the guard house, awaiting execution.

First Line: It's my wife I'm thinking of. Will she ever know the truth?

Writing

1 Write a letter to either the mother of a young man who has been shot for cowardice, or to his wife. You can write either from the perspective of:
   - an officer whose point of view is sympathetic
   - a member of the firing squad
   - one of the soldiers who witnessed the execution
   - a War Office official who explains why she will not receive a pension.

2 Imagine that you are Tommo. You are writing to Molly after Charlie's execution. How will you explain what happened?

3 Write a letter to the newspapers. You might support the execution of those showing cowardice or deserting in the face of the enemy, or you might want to object to this way of dealing with soldiers who were exhausted and shell-shocked.

DRAMATISING A COURT MARTIAL.

Read the extract from the novel of *Private Peaceful* below, as well as the poem 'The Deserter'. These extracts, as well as others in these resources, may help with the exercises that follow.

I try to close my mind to what is happening this minute to Charlie. I just try to think of Charlie as he was at home, as we all were. But all I can see in my mind are the soldiers leading Charlie out into the field. He is not stumbling. He is not struggling. He is not crying out. He is walking with his head held high, just as he was after Mr Munnings caned him at school that day. Maybe there's a lark rising, or a great crow wheeling into the wind above him. The firing squad stands at ease, waiting. Six men, their rifles loaded and ready, each one only wanting to get it over with. They will be shooting one of their own and it feels to them like murder. They try not to look at Charlie's face.

Charlie is tied to the post. The padre says a prayer, makes the sign of the cross on his forehead and moves away. It is cold but Charlie doesn't shiver. The officer, his revolver drawn, is looking at his watch. They try to put a hood over Charlie's head, but he will not have it. He looks up to the sky and sends his last living thoughts back home.

"Present! Ready! Aim!"

He closes his eyes and waits as he sings softly. "Oranges and Lemons, say the bells of St Clements." Under my breath I sing it with him. I hear the echoing volley. It is done. It is over. With that volley a part of me has died with him. I turn back to go to the solitude of my hay barn, and I find I am far from alone in my grieving. All over the camp I see them standing to attention outside their tents. And the birds are singing.

The Deserter

'I'm sorry I done it, Major'.
We bandaged the livid face;
And led him out, 'ere the wan sun rose,
To die his death of disgrace.

The bolt-heads locked to the cartridge;
The rifles steadied to rest,
As cold stock nestled at colder cheek.
And foresight lined on the breast.

'Fire!' called the Sergeant-Major.
The muzzles flamed as he spoke
And the shameless soul of a nameless man
Went up in the cordite-smoke.

By Gilbert Frankau

1 Choral Speaking

Work in a group of five or six and read the poem carefully.
Divide up the lines among the group. You may choose
one person to be the prisoner and another to be the
Sergeant-Major. Experiment with different people in the
group reading one or more lines, or even single words.
Listen carefully to the effect of the different voices as they
blend together.

Create a tableau or freeze-frame of the execution,
showing the physical attitudes and responses of the
participants. If you are working with a larger group, half
your number might present the tableau while the others
recite the poem.

2 Dream Sequence

Work in a large group. Use any of the information in this section to create a dream sequence of an execution. Remember that dreams are rarely like real life. Movement may be exaggerated and sounds distorted. You might add music or sound effects to create a nightmarish quality.

3 Creating a documentary

Working in groups, choose one aspect of World War One that you'd like to explore further. You might concentrate on life in Flanders, or present the experiences of underage soldiers. The changes to life at home in Britain might interest you, or the contribution of women to the war.

You could select and present your material as if everything was taking place in the present, actually during the war itself, or you might choose to portray the war from the perspective of the present day. Your work could be presented formally or informally as a piece of devised drama or as a radio or TV documentary.

- Reread some of the extracts and poems in these notes.
- Include items from your own research, for example diaries and letters, as well as selecting from some of the material presented here.
- Look up copies of old newspapers from the era in your local library.
- Consider the effect of the war on your locality and examine local war memorials for the names of individual soldiers.
- Whether you choose to set your documentary in the past or view it from the perspective of the 21st century, any individual voices you include will be more effective if they speak as if they are living through the event.
- Include sound effects and popular music of the time.

continued

CHILD SOLDIERS

Young soldiers from the Congolese Rebel Movement Group.

In 1990, the United Nations Convention on the Rights of the Child came into force. Article 38 aims to make sure nations take 'all feasible measures' to ensure that those under 15 do not take a direct part in hostilities and take 'all feasible measures' to ensure the protection and care of children who are affected by an armed conflict.

In spite of these aims, around 300,000 children, some as young as seven, are fighting in wars around the world. Most are boys, but girls are also forced to fight. The Democratic Republic of Congo has been embroiled in civil war since 1998. There are an estimated 10–20,000 boys under the age of 18 fighting for all armed groups in the civil war. Both government and rebel armies use child soldiers. Some children see fighting as the only way to escape from poverty. Even the offer of regular food is enough to make some sign up.

Francisco and Adriana live in a secret rehabilitation centre for child soldiers in Bogota. Both children were recruited to the front lines in Colombia's civil war. Francisco is 13. Francisco said his parents had urged him to join up, *"because they said I would get a good meal every day and some clothes."* He killed a policeman with a hand grenade. He ran away from the guerrillas because he wanted to see his mother. His parents greeted his return with horror and told him to give himself up to the army. Instead he went into hiding. The guerrillas kill all deserters, no matter what their age.

Adriana is 17. She is a veteran of five years service with the Marxist guerrillas of the Revolutionary Armed Forces of Colombia (FARC), which began when she was 11.

"I took part in two attacks, one on a police station and another on an army base. I just remember the wounded, some of them my friends. One was hit everywhere, there were bits of grenade all through his body. The worse thing was that he didn't die. I can't really leave here. I am marked, and cannot walk out on the streets. There are guerrillas everywhere and they will kill me. I just can't relax, I cannot visit my family, because it's so dangerous."

All the children at the rehab centre volunteered to join the guerrillas. Most of them are from peasant families living well below the poverty line. Columbia's problems will not end with peace. After 37 years of civil conflict three generations of children have grown up amid horrific violence.

Movement

Situation: Either Francisco or Adriana represent the Hunted. One of the guerrillas is the Hunter, whose task is to discover them.

Organisation: Work as a whole group. The group stands in a large circle. The Hunter and the Hunted are blindfolded. The rest of the group must try to protect the players from bumping into objects or leaving the circle. When the players start to move, the rest of the group must remain completely still. The Hunter tries to finds the Hunted by listening carefully for any sounds.

Movement Extension: One of you is either Adriana or Francisco. You need to return to your family – perhaps one of your parents or siblings is ill. The rest of the class stand in a large circle with their backs turned. Can you cross the room without being heard by the others?

Role-play Extension: If you are stopped by the guerillas, try to explain who you are and what you are doing. Can you persuade them to allow you to continue your journey?

WAR MEMORIALS

The National Memorial Arboretum near Lichfield was created in remembrance of those who lost their lives in the service of their country. In 2001 a statue to commemorate those who were shot at dawn for cowardice and desertion in the First World War was unveiled by the daughter of Harry Farr.

"If the dead could march, side by side in continuous procession down Whitehall, it would take them four days and nights to get past the saluting base".

Alan Clark

Drama

- Work in a group of five or six. Create 3 statues that depict:
  1 a group of young soldiers in World War 1
  2 Charlie Peaceful
  3 a group of child soldiers in the present day

- Present your statues to the rest of the class. What differences do they notice in the attitudes represented in each?

- Compare your statues with examples of real war memorials.

Research and Discussion

The statue of Field Marshal Douglas Haig stands proudly in Whitehall, celebrating a victory which cost the lives of many thousands of brave soldiers who died in the trenches of the Somme and Passchendaele. Some military historians believe that hundreds of thousands of soldiers died needlessly as a result of Haig's orders. Others have praised Haig, arguing that he did well under the circumstances.

- Do some research (in the library and on the Internet) into the career of Field Marshal Haig.

- Is it right that a statue should honour Field Marshal Haig?

- Would a memorial of one of the ordinary soldiers who lost their lives in the war be more appropriate, or is the Cenotaph, dedicated to The Unknown Soldier, a sufficient memorial?

The statue of Field Marshal Haig overlooked by Edinburgh Castle.

The General

'Good-morning; good-morning!' the General said
When we met him last week on our way to the line.
Now the soldiers he smiled at are most of them dead,
And we're cursing his staff for incompetent swine.
'He's a cheery old card,' grunted Harry to Jack
As they slogged up to Arras with rifle and pack.

But he did for them both by his plan of attack.

Siegfried Sassoon

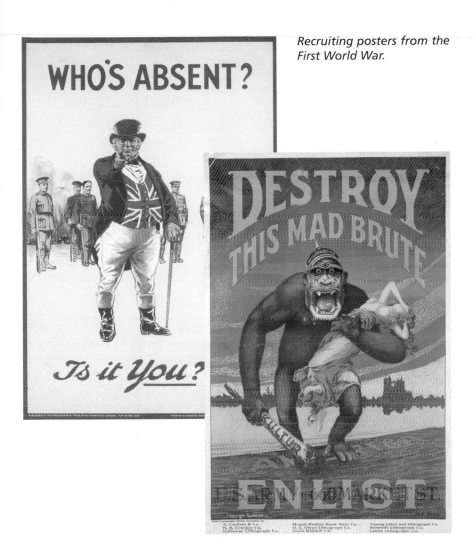

Recruiting posters from the First World War.

PROPAGANDA AND THE MEDIA

There were strong government controls on press reporting during the First World War. There were no images of dead bodies and little mention of shell-shock, military discipline and conditions in the trenches. At first photographers and journalists were prevented visiting the Front, but later official war artists and photographers were appointed to record the war.

In every war propaganda is designed to promote loyalty, unity and pride and to stir up feelings against the enemy. The courage and patriotism of significant public figures – politicians, royalty, celebrities – are highlighted and their images used to bolster public support for the struggle. Every aspect of the media – newspapers, TV, radio, films, posters, cartoons and most recently the internet have been exploited to influence people's opinions.

Propaganda works by:

- Concealing unwelcome facts.
- Down-playing the realities of the war.
- Censoring the media.
- Emphasising the justice of the cause.
- Highlighting the need to defend a way of life and possessions, as well as rights and freedoms.
- Using language and images to arouse hatred for the enemy
- Depicting the enemy as diabolical or inhuman.
- Spreading stories of atrocities.
- Intensifying the threat of persecution and death.
- Using mockery and sarcasm to insult or ridicule the enemy.

Discussion and Research

- Propaganda is not always limited to wartime. Do you think that governments are right to use propaganda to gain support for their policies?

- Look at a recent newspaper. Can you find any items which could be described as propaganda?

- Research a particular subject – perhaps a recent war or a controversial government policy – and discover how it has been handled in the media.

- Do you believe that important people, including royalty, are really allowed to suffer the same danger and hardships as ordinary people?

Writing and research

Choose a subject about which you feel strongly – either supporting it or opposing it. You might pick some topic which is currently in the news – animal rights, genetic research, the environment, euthanasia, etc.

- Research your topic in the media and on the internet.

- Try to identify the kinds of strategies used by those presenting evidence for or against your topic.

- Write a piece of propaganda, using some relevant tactics from those listed above.

- Make a speech using your arguments to try to gain support for your point of view.

Further Resources

Search the internet for information about the First World War. There are many websites which outline the background and progress of the war, include photographic images and personal documents. Explore the following sites to research particular topics.

Websites

www.iwm.org.uk

www.firstworldwar.com

www.bbc.co.uk/history

If you have the opportunity, visit the Imperial War Museum in London where The Trench Experience re-creates conditions in a World War 1 trench.

Films

Two films dealing with the First World War and available on DVD:

All Quiet on the Western Front – 1930   Director: Lewis Milestone

One of the most powerful anti-war films ever made, it shows the German perspective on the war. It was denounced and banned by the Nazis during World War II.

> *"This story is neither an accusation nor a confession, and least of all an adventure, for death is not an adventure to those who stand face to face with it. It will try simply to tell of a generation of men who, even though they may have escaped its shells, were destroyed by the war…"*

Paths of Glory – 1957   Director: Stanley Kubrick

When French soldiers refuse to continue with an impossible attack, their superiors decide to make an example of them and execute three randomly-chosen innocent men. The film was banned in France and Switzerland for almost twenty years following its release.

Play

The play *Journey's End* by R.C. Sheriff was first performed in 1928. It is based on the author's experiences in the war and focuses on the lives of five officers waiting in a trench during the three days in 1918. It was made into a film in 1930 and a TV version was broadcast in 1988.